The Judy Garland Collector's Guide

Edward R. Pardella

4880 Lower Valley Road, Atglen, PA 19310 USA

Dedication

For Joseph Denofrio. Your positive encouragement and advice, once again, have been invaluable. I will remain forever grateful for the patience you displayed while listening to each and every draft of this manuscript, read aloud, from its conception to final draft.

For Woolsey Ackerman and Michael Siewert. Your kindness and generosity helped make this book possible. Thank you so much.

And for Judy. I hope this book, in some way, begins to express the gratitude I feel for the pleasure that your motion pictures have brought to me throughout my life.

Copyright © 1999 by Edward R. Pardella
Photographed by Philip Isaiah Katz
Library of Congress Catalog Card Number: 98-88916

Book Design by Anne Davidsen
Type set in BerhardMod BT/GoudyOISt BT

ISBN: 0-7643-0764-9
Printed in China
1 2 3 4

Published by Schiffer Publishing Ltd.
4880 Lower Valley Road
Atglen, PA 19310
Phone: (610) 593-1777; Fax: (610) 593-2002
E-mail: Schifferbk@aol.com
Please visit our web site catalog at www.schifferbooks.com

This book may be purchased from the publisher.
Include $3.95 for shipping.
Please try your bookstore first.
We are interested in hearing from authors
with book ideas on related subjects.
You may write for a free catalog.

In Europe, Schiffer books are distributed by
Bushwood Books
6 Marksbury Rd.
Kew Gardens
Surrey TW9 4JF England
Phone: 44 (0) 181 392-8585; Fax: 44 (0) 181 392-9876
E-mail: Bushwd@aol.com

Contents

Acknowledgments

Every effort has been made to correctly identify and acknowledge the publishers, manufacturers, artists, and copyright holders for the materials illustrated throughout this reference guide. In many cases, the companies no longer exist, or items such as publicity photographs are unmarked, making it virtually impossible to credit the photographer or seek permission for their use. I respectfully welcome the opportunity to make corrections or to include any unintentional omissions of information concerning ownership and copyright, should there be a reprinting or revised edition to this reference guide.

My deepest appreciation to my editor, Jennifer A. Lindbeck, and my publisher, Peter and Nancy Schiffer. Thank you for making this project a reality. I also wish to acknowledge photographer Philip Isaiah Katz, Blackfan Studio. Many thanks for your time, talent, and for a job well done.

This book would not have possible without the enormous generosity of several people. For entrusting me with their personal collections, my sincere gratitude is extended to: Woolsey Ackerman, Michael Siewert, Marge Meisinger, John C. Van Doren, Herb Millman, and Jim and Merlyn Collings.

A special word of thanks and acknowledgment to Paula Allen at Warner Bros. Worldwide Publishing/Turner Entertainment and to the staff of the Academy of Motion Picture Arts and Sciences, Margaret Herrick Library. And to the color laser specialists at Visual Miracles, Inc.

For advice, words of encouragement, or support, I am indebted to: Joseph Denofrio, David Bowers, John Fricke, Fred McFadden, Peter Levy. And for the much needed computer advice Elizabeth Majerle and Andrew Walsh.

Price Guide

Memorabilia captions will include one of the following letters to estimate an item's current dollar value.

a. $5 - 20
b. 25 - 65
c. 70 - 100
d. 100 - 150
e. 175 - 200
f. 200 - 300
g. 400 - 500
h. 500 - 1000
i. 1000 - 2000
j. 2500 +
k. 5000 + +

Please note: magazines, sheet music, and record albums will usually fall into the price **b.** category, with the exception of Oz related items, items of extreme rarity, or where otherwise indicated.

Condition, desirability, and rarity are three main factors that determine price. Condition is always of major importance and should be a top priority when making any purchase. Prices listed in this volume represent the estimated current market value (at the time of publishing) for items in mint and near mint condition and are based upon prices realized at auction houses and in the collector's market place. Neither the author nor the publisher assume any responsibility for losses incurred as a result of using this price guide. Prices listed are NOT intended to set prices, but rather to act and ONLY act as a guide. Prices may vary regionally throughout the country.

Biography

From Gumm to Garland

Judy Garland's legendary "born-in-a-trunk" career began in the small rural logging town of Grand Rapids, Minnesota. Her parents, Frank and Ethel Gumm, owned and operated the town's silent movie theater, the New Grand. Frank was manager and ticket-taker, while Ethel accompanied the silent films on piano. It was here, on the stage of the New Grand, that the legend began and a star was born.

Literally, growing up watching movies with a guaranteed front row seat, Judy sat in her parent's theater night after night mesmerized by the screen's flickering, soundless, black and white images. Like her parents, she was soon well on her way toward a total love affair with the movies, and with the tiny motion picture community, nestled tightly in the foothills of Southern California, called Hollywood.

At the time of her birth, in 1922, Hollywood was already firmly established as the motion picture capital of the world. Churning out nearly 800 films a year, the tiny, sun-drenched community surrounded by endless acres of avocado and citrus groves had quickly grown into more than just another town, more than just the center of the American film industry. Hollywood was now a total state of mind, an envied magical world, of luxury and glamour, fantasy and un-imagined spectacle. It was a place where, for the 15¢ price of admission, all of your dreams could come true and absolutely anything seemed possible.

By the early 1920s, giant motion picture palaces had replaced the nickelodeons of the turn-of-the-century, and audiences had now discovered that along with the movies came movie stars. The "It Girl" Clara Bow and seductive screen sirens Theda Bara and Gloria Swanson vamped their way through naughty-but-nice flapper movies, while comedians Charlie Chaplin, Harold Lloyd, and Buster Keaton took pies in the face and slipped on banana peels. Tom Mix, Hoot Gibson, and Harry Carey tamed the wild west as the screen's most famous cowboys, while female audience members swooned over the dashing young swashbuckler Douglas Fairbanks and "The Sheik" Rudolph Valentino.

The film industry's newly emerging star system also provided moviegoers with their first child star. She was "the girl with the golden hair," Mary Pickford. Following quickly on the heels of Mary's success were child stars Jackie Coogan, Baby Peggy, and a mischievous cast of "little rascals," the *Our Gang.* Together, their motion pictures launched the beginnings of a baby boom explosion on the film industry that Hollywood would never forget. Suddenly, every studio in town was frantically searching for their own child star sensation. Star-struck parents, from every corner of the country, quickly packed up their belongings and, with "Baby" in tow, began heading west for California. Throughout the 1920s and 30s, an estimated 1,000 children a day poured steadily into the studios and streets of Hollywood, all hoping to be "discovered," hoping to become a "star." Among them was a young hopeful named Judy Garland.

Given the name Frances Ethel Gumm, Judy was born nearly two weeks late on Saturday, June 10, 1922, at approximately 5:30 a.m. Weighing an even 7 pounds, she had dark brown hair and deep set dark brown eyes. In the weeks following her birth, everyone was quick to agree that the tiny infant just didn't seem to look like a Frances. Her sisters, Mary Jane and Virginia (nick-named Susie and Jimmy), soon began calling her "Baby," which somehow seemed to fit. From that moment on, she was referred to by everyone as Baby, later shortened to Babe.

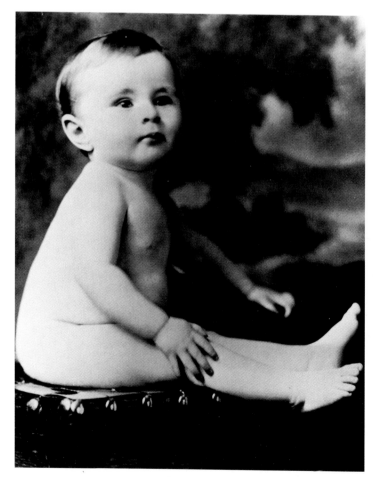

Frances Ethel Gumm, 1923.

With the newest member of the Gumm family at her side, Ethel Gumm resumed her position back at the piano, while Frank now began introducing his audience members to a series of weekly amateur nights, every Friday at 9 p.m. The New Grand also had an added attraction of (daughters) Mary Jane and Virginia singing and performing together as the Gumm Sisters. Their popularity in the amateur nights made them welcomed regulars to the stage of the Grand, and their appearances were soon expanded to two nights a week with a Sunday matinee.

While carefully being taught the words to "Jingle Bells," Baby was fashioned with a tiny costume of white cotton and lace. Her sisters added their contribution, with a small sprig of holly pinned to her dress for good luck. After a few last minute words of instruction, she was ready. At age two and a half, she made her stage debut on December 26, 1924, between showings of the motion picture *Through The Back Door*, starring Mary Pickford.

Baby Gumm, circa 1924.

Baby in her theatrical debut costume. Christmas, 1924.

With Frank leading the applause, the Gumm Sister's act was patterned after the girl's favorite singing sister act of the day—the Duncan Sisters, Vivian and Rosetta. They sang all of the Duncan Sisters' hit songs, followed by several dance routines. The act was proudly choreographed, costumed, and accompanied on the piano by Ethel.

Billing themselves as Jack and Virginia Lee, Sweet Southern Singers Frank and Ethel Gumm were no strangers to the world of show business, having performed together along the vaudeville circuits of the upper Midwest. Ethel had always loved music and performing, but it was Frank, she said, who was truly "stage-struck," claiming he had "show business in his blood." It seemed only natural to them that their children would somehow follow in their footsteps. Even two-year-old Baby wanted to get into the act.

Sitting in the audience watching her sisters perform each night, Baby tried desperately, from the time she could barely walk, to run up on stage and join the singing and dancing. After nearly succeeding in her attempts to reach the footlights on several occasions, Ethel realized that Baby could not be contained for much longer. She pleaded night after night, "Mama, I want to sing too!" It was finally decided that she would be included as the surprise finale in the New Grand's annual Christmas program.

After joining her sisters for the final chorus of "When My Sugar Walks Down the Street," carrying a little silver bell that she had been taught to ring at the appropriate times throughout her solo, Baby bounced daringly, with neither a hint of apprehension or shyness, to center stage. Confident and proud, she took a bow and began to sing at the very top of her powerful lungs. When her song was finished, she took another bow, smiled sweetly, and quickly started again, from the top: "Jingle Bells, Jingle Bells." As the applause, now mixed with laughter, grew louder, Baby continued to sing, chorus after chorus. Finally, after nearly reaching the end of her fifth chorus, Grandma Eva (Ethel's mother) leaped onto the stage, scooped her up into her arms, and carried her off. She waved good-bye and together they disappeared into the wings. The audience, charmed by Baby's show-stopping antics, could still hear her little silver bell ringing from backstage. Their applause grew even louder, and Baby's debut literally brought down the house. It seemed that there were now three singing Gumm Sisters, with Baby Gumm as the feature.

Over the next year and a half, Baby appeared with her sisters on the stage of the New Grand, at local town events and store openings, as well as several performances at theaters in the surrounding area. In the summer of 1926, the Gumm family left Grand Rapids for a three-month vaudeville tour, which, upon completion, would help finance a weeks vacation in California. Again billing themselves as Jack and Virginia Lee, Frank and Ethel now expanded their act to include, singing in three part harmony, the Three Little Lees. Together, they worked their way across the country to San Francisco, where they quickly boarded a train for Los Angeles for a much anticipated vacation. "We had a wonderful time," Ethel would later recall. "We walked our fool heads off, camped on the lawn of the old Warner Studio on Sunset Boulevard, and watched the stars come out. But what Frank and I really loved was the climate: roses and balmy skies, even in the middle of winter. This was the place we decided; this was it." Following a final, farewell performance in Grand Rapids, Frank sold the New Grand and the family headed west to sunny California, where Judy recalled, "Jackie Coogan and the *Our Gang* comedies had inspired mother."

Reaching Los Angeles, Frank and Ethel quickly discovered that all of the movie theaters were owned and operated by large corporations or by the motion picture studios themselves. With few alternatives for employment, they eventually settled seventy-five miles northeast of Hollywood, in the Mojave Desert community of Lancaster. Frank leased the Antelope Valley Theater and the Gumm Sisters were soon back on stage, with evening performances at 9 p.m. and a Sunday matinee.

Ethel now began driving her daughters into Hollywood each weekend for professional singing and dancing lessons. With well packaged, live stage shows, promising "101 Meglin Wonder Kiddies, Kute, Klever, and Kunning," they would begin at the Ethel Meglin Studio, Hollywood's most successful showcase for child actors. To help pay for her daughter's tuition, Ethel Gumm assumed the position of rehearsal pianist, and the Gumm Sisters quickly became featured performers in the Meglin Kiddie Shows. Making several appearances at the Orpheum and Loew's State theaters, in downtown Los Angeles, Baby, dressed as Cupid, was showcased singing "I Can't Give You Anything But Love."

In June of 1929, the Gumm Sisters made their motion picture debut with the Meglin Kiddies, in a one-reel film short entitled *The Big Revue* (Mayfair Pictures). Featured in a song and dance number entitled "The Good Old Sunny South," their screen debut was not exactly memorable, but notable for the genuine enthusiasm and apparent ease with which seven-year-old Baby performed. Stealing all of the attention from her two older sisters, she provided audiences with their first hint of her powerful voice and enormous raw talent. In 1930, the Gumm Sisters appeared in three more film shorts including *A Holiday in Storyland*, *The Wedding of Jack and Jill*, and *Bubbles* (First National Vitaphone Pictures).

The Gumm Sisters, Mary Jane, Virginia, and Baby, as they appeared in their motion picture debut *The Big Revue*, 1929.

By 1930, the Gumm Sisters act would showcase Baby with solo performances of "I Can't Give You Anything But Love" and "My Mammy."

With the act now clearly showcasing Baby's vocal talent, the next few years brought the Gumm Sisters continued stage success and several semi-regular radio appearances on programs such as *The Kiddies Hour* (KFI) and *The Junior Hi-Jinx Hour* (KFWB). One of Baby's most noteworthy engagements during this period was in January and March of 1932, when she made a series of nightclub appearances at the world famous Coconut Grove, in Hollywood. Reviewers labeled her "Little Miss Leather Lungs," and her rendition of Helen Morgan's hit song "Bill" brought her recognition as "The Little Girl with the Big Voice."

In 1934, the Gumm Sisters were back on the road again, this time performing together at Chicago's Oriental theater. The show's head liner and emcee was comedian

George Jessel. Jessel opened the show surrounded by a line of chorus girls, followed by the Gumm Sisters, who appeared second on the bill. As Jessel introduced the girls for the first show, he got a huge laugh from the audience. He had mistakenly thought that they were a comedy act, so he really punched the name Gumm. The girls came on and, of course, they were not funny at all. Their smooth, three-part harmonies and polished performance literally stopped the show. Jessel was horrified that his introduction had gotten a laugh. He told them, "You have got to change your name!" Later that day, after receiving a phone call from Robert Garland, a theater critic from the *New York World Telegram*, Jessel thought that being named after an important drama critic might help the girls' career. For the next show, he introduced the Gumm Sisters as the "Garland Sisters."

In an effort to drop her out-grown nickname of Baby, Frances soon coined a new first name as well. Previous billing changes included among others: Baby Gumm, Baby Frances, Frances Gumm, Baby Marie Gumm, Alice Gumm, and even Gracie Gumm. With the help of Hoagie Carmichael's current hit song "Judy," she was now Judy Garland.

Susie, Jimmy, and Judy. The Garland Sisters, 1934.

The Road to Oz

There are several conflicting stories as to how and when Judy Garland was first brought to the attention of Metro-Goldwyn-Mayer and its vice president in charge of production Louis B. Mayer. It appears to have happened something like this: Judy was playing in her backyard one day, when they received an unexpected call saying that they wanted to hear her sing at MGM; her father decided to take her to the audition just as she was: no frilly dress, no hair ribbons, just her regular play clothes, dirty face and all. She sang "Zing! Went The Strings of My Heart." After she had finished, Mayer left without saying a word. Judy and her father both thought the audition was a big nothing, so they went home and tried to forget about it. Two weeks later, she was under contract, without a screen test.

Judy Garland's first studio contract was officially approved on October 13, 1935. However, her extraordinary fifteen-year association with Metro-Goldwyn-Mayer began with much uncertainty. Almost immediately upon her arrival, she found herself involved in an unexpected sequence of events surrounding another promising young singer named Edna Mae (Deanna) Durbin.

The two girls had each arrived at Metro in the fall of 1935, when the "Tiffany of Studios" was at its peek of production and prestige. Producing a record fifty-two films a year, the studio spanned an area nearly two miles long, stretching over 117 acres of pure movie magic, just west of Los Angeles,

in nearby Culver City. With Louis B. Mayer at the helm, the studio was dedicated to producing the finest, most technically superior product possible. At the heart of MGM was its unchallenged roster of 235 contract players, boasted proudly by the slogan "More Stars Than There Are In The Heavens." The impressive list included among others: Ethel, John, and Lionel Barrymore; Wallace Berry; Jackie Cooper; Joan Crawford; Nelson Eddy; Clark Gable; Greta Garbo; Jean Harlow; Helen Hayes; Laurel and Hardy; Myrna Loy; Jeanette MacDonald; Robert Montgomery; Frank Morgan; Maureen O'Sullivan; Eleanor Powell; William Powell; Norma Shearer; Spencer Tracy; and Johnny Weismuller.

As Metro's newest acquisitions, Judy and Deanna were immediately assigned to the studio's rigorous grooming process. They began early each morning with the finest professional training in singing, dancing, diction, makeup, and hairdressing, followed by three hours of academic schooling at the studio's little red school house.

At a starting salary of $100 per week, the girls were each signed to a standard long-term contract, with several six-month option clauses, which the studio could pick-up or drop at any time. From the very beginning, the future of both girls seemed rather uncertain. Louis B. Mayer was immediately pressured by the New York office to release one of them. It was felt that one, new, young, singing sensation was enough on the growing studio roster. The problem was who would stay and who would go? Mayer and his advisors felt certain that teaming the girls against one another would best enable them to decide.

The ball was started rolling on a project entitled *Every Sunday*. Owned by MGM for some time, the story was slated to become a full-length feature film someday. However, for now, it would serve as a quickly tailored short-subject, to fit the talents of the two very different young girls.

Deanna, six-months older than Judy, was an elegant child who possessed a rare, unspoiled quality of sweetness and innocence. At fourteen years old, she was graceful and charming and was quickly blossoming into a delicate young beauty.

California's Child Welfare laws dictated that several hours each day would be set aside for the education of Hollywood's movie children. However, contract players under the age of eighteen, such as Mickey Rooney and Judy Garland, shown here in front of MGM's little red schoolhouse in early 1937, attended classes only when time permitted. Movie studios seldom, if ever, properly educated their young stars, for they were far more valuable in front of the camera than behind a desk. For Mickey and Judy, the lessons that were eventually taught were most often done under nearly impossible conditions—on the set, in-between takes.

Her well-trained operatic singing style and dazzling smile were much favored by Louis B. Mayer, who had always fancied himself as a connoisseur of opera and beauty.

Compared to Deanna Durbin, Judy, on the other hand, seemed rather rough and unpolished. At thirteen years old, she was slightly over weight, with her hair and clothing always managing to somehow look as if she just stepped right out of a windstorm. Having a tremendous sense of humor, she was an endless bundle of energy and enthusiasm. At the slightest provocation she would explode into a wave of uncontrollable laughter. With wild impersonations of everyone and everything continually pouring out of her, she appeared always to be out of breath. Wrinkling her nose for added punctuation, it looked as if at any moment she would simply burst at the seams! Her remarkably mature singing voice was well showcased by her jazzy style and by her years of experience performing on stage as a member of the Gumm Sisters. Both girls were uniquely talented, but totally opposite. So the competition was set—Opera versus Jazz, Deanna Durbin versus Judy Garland.

The simple storyline for *Every Sunday* centered around an outdoor band concert, which, if successful, would help save a public park from being destroyed by developers. Filming took less than a week to complete, with just four days to prepare the songs, script, and costumes. However, before the finished product could be readied for viewing Mayer was summoned out of the country on studio business and promotion. Returning several weeks later, he immediately ordered a screening. With advisors at his side, he sat quietly as the film unfolded. When the lights came up at the end, he stood and announced, "We'll keep them both!"

Contract players Deanna Durbin and Judy Garland, behind the scenes on the set of *Every Sunday*, 1936.

9

Every Sunday was now slated to be produced into a full-length feature film, with Judy Garland and Deanna Durbin starring together as Metro-Goldwyn-Mayer's newest musical team. Unfortunately, during Mayer's absence from the studio, Metro had somehow failed to pick up Deanna's renewal clause, so her option was dropped. Without hesitation, she was quickly snatched away by Joseph Pasternak and Universal Pictures. Pasternak had tried earlier that same year to obtain the services of Judy on a loan-out basis to star in a musical he was preparing, entitled *Three Smart Girls*. Metro refused the request, so now, with Deanna Durbin suddenly available, the film was repackaged and tailored especially for her. Mayer was furious over the loss of his operatic protégée, but remained determined, perhaps now more than ever, to prove that his decision to keep Judy Garland under contract was a sound and profitable one.

Judy spent the next several months at MGM, continuing with her professional training and grooming, without her much anticipated, first feature film assignment. Instead, she was kept busy performing on the radio and making personal appearances for studio promotion. Without a definite idea as to how, when, or where she would initially be used, Metro-Goldwyn-Mayer executives remained optimistic that with the right training and given the right opportunity the awkward looking teenager was somehow destined for greatness and stardom.

Throughout the 1930s and 40s, radio provided MGM with a perfect promotional vehicle to showcase up-coming films, introduce new songs, and test new talent. Contract player Judy Garland, shown here, makes a guest appearance on the radio program *Jack Oakie's College*, 1937.

On the set of the motion picture *Parnell*, starring Clark Gable, Judy Garland sings "Dear Mr. Gable, You Made Me Love You" to Hollywood's king, 1937.

In July of 1936, with still no film projects scheduled for her at MGM, Judy was loaned to 20th Century-Fox studios for a supporting role in their collegiate football, musical comedy production *Pigskin Parade*. Starring Stuart Erwin, Jack Haley, and Betty Grable, the film marked Judy's debut into feature films. Unfortunately, it was not the sort of debut that she had hoped for.

Cast as a pigtailed, hillbilly girl named Sairy Dodd, Judy's role was small and far from the glamorous beginning that she had imagined. At a special studio preview, she sat with her mother and anxiously awaited the start of the picture. Judy watched as she made her first appearance nearly an hour into the film, projected larger than life before her very eyes. She hoped that she might look as beautiful as Garbo or Crawford, that the makeup and lighting would automatically make her look glamorous. After seeing herself on the screen, Judy commented that it was the most awful moment in her life. "I was fat," she recalled. "A fat little pig in pigtails. My acting was terrible. I was just little kick-the-can Baby Gumm."

Returning to Metro, things finally began to look up for Judy when she literally stole-the-show in her first full-length MGM motion picture—the star-studded *Broadway Melody of 1938*. Singing to a scrapbook filled with photographs of Clark Gable, with special music and lyrics written by one of Metro's top musical arrangers Roger Edens, she was featured singing "(Dear Mr. Gable) You Made Me Love You." Edens had created the number originally for Judy to perform at a special surprise party for Clark Gable's thirty-sixth birthday. The song was well received, bringing Gable to tears and Judy

Garland to the attention of the studio's top brass. "(Dear Mr. Gable) You Made Me Love You" and a featured role as Sophie Tucker's daughter were now quickly worked into *Broadway Melody*, which was already under production. Reviewers singled her out as "sensational" and "amazing," with the *Los Angeles Herald-Express* reporting that Judy "walks away with the picture." At last, she was on her way.

There were now featured roles in four more quick films over the next year and a half including: *Thoroughbreds Don't Cry* (1937), the first of nine successful ventures playing opposite Mickey Rooney; *Everybody Sing* (1938) with Fanny Brice; *Listen, Darling* (1938), playing opposite young Freddie Bartholomew; and the third installment in the wholesome, light-hearted Andy Hardy series starring Mickey Rooney, entitled *Love Finds Andy Hardy* (1938). Finally, in 1939 came the starring role of Dorothy Gale in *The Wizard of Oz*.

The enormous box office success of Walt Disney's first full-length, animated feature film *Snow White and the Seven Dwarfs* sent motion picture producers throughout Hollywood scrambling to find other children's stories and fairytales as possible future projects. The most obvious candidate (at the time) was the classic L. Frank Baum fantasy adventure *The Wonderful Wizard of Oz*. Five major studios bid for the rights to the property, including 20th Century-Fox, hoping to acquire the film as a possible vehicle for Shirley Temple. The bidding war ended with Metro-Goldwyn-Mayer's offer of $75,000.

Judy Garland as she appeared in her original hair, makeup, and wardrobe tests for her role as Dorothy Gale in *The Wizard of Oz*.

On February 24, 1938, gossip columnist Louella Parsons reported Metro's purchase of *The Wizard of Oz*, headlining "Judy Garland To Play Dorothy." MGM's parent company, Loew's Incorporated voiced objections to the choice of Garland for the role as Dorothy from the very beginning. They cited the need for a proven box office star for the studio's most expensive production to date.

Reportedly, Louis B. Mayer approached Darryl F. Zanuck, the head of Fox studios, hoping to negotiate a deal for the services of Shirley Temple to play Dorothy; however, the request was refused. In addition, there were a few limited discussions as to the possibility of using Universal's number one attraction Deanna Durbin or perhaps even Bonita Granville from Warner Bros.; though, *Oz* producer Mervyn LeRoy had his own idea as to who should play the lead role of Dorothy. His insistence eventually prevailed, and Judy Garland soon began her fantastic journey down the Yellow Brick Road.

As producer of Metro-Goldwyn-Mayer's most ambitious undertaking to date, Mervyn LeRoy was given the opportunity, budget, and luxury of assembling the finest staff of skilled artisans, technicians, and performers that Hollywood had to offer. Preparations began immediately, with over seven months of pre-production work to follow, as script, score, casting, set construction, and the film's groundbreaking special-effects were being developed. Extensive wardrobe fittings and makeup tests were also scheduled. Detailed character design concepts were created and refined for all of the whimsical inhabitants of *Oz*. Judy Garland underwent several weeks of hair, makeup, and costume revisions before filming actually got under way sometime in mid October of 1938.

With Judy's chest tightly bound to hide her maturing, sixteen-year-old figure, costume designer Gilbert Adrian created no less than six different original dress designs for her, while makeup artist Jack Dawn developed almost as many choices for her hair style and color. Weeks of fittings and wardrobe tests followed before Mervyn LeRoy was finally satisfied and ready to begin.

When principal photography began on *The Wizard of Oz*, Judy Garland appeared on screen with long blond hair and was costumed in a solid blue jumper, trimmed with polka-dotted details (see chapter on Costumes). The finished result was highly stylized, leaving Judy almost completely unrecognizable. Looking extremely fanciful for a simple Kansas farm girl, the entire original costume, hair, and makeup were quickly discarded after only two weeks of filming. Judy Garland would later recall that she "looked like a male Mary Pickford by the time they got through with the alterations."

The production had other problems from the start as well: the most important of which centered around the film's director Richard Thorpe. At first, he had appeared to be ideally suited for the enormous task of bringing *The Wizard of Oz* to the screen. He was chosen to direct the picture for his reputation of completing films on schedule and under budget. What he reportedly lacked, however, was a distinct personal style. He also had somehow failed to grasp a clear understanding of the story behind the *Oz* script and for the warmth and feeling that was envisioned for the film. He was fired after only twelve days of shooting.

Dissatisfied with the entire Thorpe footage, LeRoy decided to start all over again, from scratch. Director George Cukor was now brought in, and he immediately ordered new wardrobe and makeup tests for Dorothy and several of the other principal characters. Cukor's brief, but tremendous contribution to the film at this stage was highly instrumental for the final success of the motion picture; his results provided the polished, finished look that the main characters ultimately displayed on screen.

Special attention was now also given to Judy Garland's performance. A subtle believability and sincerity was essential for the part of Dorothy. Up until this point, her portrayal, as directed by Thorpe, had been "over-the-top" and artificial. Cukor reminded Judy that Dorothy was after all "just a little girl from Kansas." After completing the desperately needed makeup and wardrobe changes, and due to previous commitments, Cukor now was no longer available or interested in continuing work on the project. On October 31, 1938, Victor Fleming was officially announced as director of *The Wizard of Oz*.

Soon, a whirling cyclone would whisk Dorothy and her dog, Toto, from their drab, black and white existence in Kansas to an extraordinary technicolor adventure "Over the Rainbow." Dreaming of a land called *Oz*, Dorothy envisions witches that fly on broomsticks, little people called Munchkins that sing and dance, trees that talk, and poppies that put you to sleep. In search of the great and powerful Wizard of Oz, she journeys down the Yellow Brick Road to the Emerald City, accompanied by a Scarecrow who is searching for a brain, a Tin Man in search of a heart, and a Cowardly Lion hoping to find his courage. Eventually, a pair of magical ruby slippers return her to her home and family, where she awakens and realizes that "there's no place like home."

Receiving critical acclaim nationwide, *The Wizard of Oz* premiered in Los Angeles, on August 15, 1939. Of Judy Garland's performance, Louella Parsons wrote "This is little Judy Garland's great triumph and the best thing she has ever done." The *Hollywood Spectator* reported "the outstanding feature of the production is the astonishingly clever performance of Judy Garland, holding the picture together, being always its motivating feature, and so natural is she, so perfectly cast." The *Chicago Daily Tribune* noted "Judy Garland was a perfect choice for Dorothy. She portrays, without a false move, an honest-to-goodness little girl, genuinely flabbergasted, curious, terrified, game, lonely, ecstatic, as the case may call for—and you're just going to love her." *Picture Reports* printed "Garland deserves stardom for her performance."

In her role as Dorothy in *The Wizard of Oz*, Judy Garland had suddenly found her place in motion picture history. At the Twelfth Annual Academy Awards ceremony, held on February 29, 1940, she was presented with a special miniature Oscar ™ as the year's "best juvenile performer."[1] Stardom was officially secured with the placing of her hand and foot prints in cement in the forecourt of Grauman's Chinese theater, leaving her forever immotalized as a member of Hollywood royalty.

The following pages will provide the reader with a rare, never before published, comprehensive, photographic record of Judy Garland's enormous professional achievements and with the merchandising that was produced as a result of her extraordinary life and career.

At the west-coast premiere of *Babes in Arms*, on October 10, 1939, Judy became the seventy-fourth star to place her hand and foot prints in cement at Grauman's Chinese theater, in Hollywood. Her inscription reads "For Mr. Grauman. All Happiness, Judy Garland."

Presented by Mickey Rooney, Judy Garland receives her special Academy Award. Previous winners of the miniature statuette included: Shirley Temple, Mickey Rooney, and Deanna Durbin.

[1] Oscar ™ is the registered trademark and service mark of the Academy of Motion Picture Arts and Sciences.

The Portrait Gallery

The process of publicizing and promoting the studio's newest acquisitions began at the MGM Portrait Gallery. The Gallery's impressive team of photographers, makeup artists, hairdressers, and fashion experts determined exactly how each new contract player would best be photographed and presented to the public: what lighting would be best and at what angles, how they would be dressed and in what colors, and the physical traits to be emphasized or suppressed; all was carefully scrutinized. Here, through the wizardry of the Gallery's technicians, each of the studio's new young starlets entered like the shy and unknown Harlean Carpentier, only later magically to emerge as a glamorous Jean Harlow. It would take more than just a lipstick and a powder puff for Judy to emerge looking anything like the seductive beauties whose portraits lined the Gallery walls. At the time of her arrival, the freckled-faced, nail-biting, giggling, thirteen year old by no means fit the mold of sophistication or glamour that was expected of a Hollywood starlet.

The Gallery's first task in regards to Judy Garland was to get her weight problem under control. It seemed that she had an incurable passion for chocolate. Anything would do: candy, ice cream, milk shakes, or cake. It didn't matter as long as it was chocolate! She was immediately placed on an exercise program, combined with a strict diet consisting of water and Louis B. Mayer's favorite—home-made chicken soup. Provided eagerly by the MGM commissary, and as instructed by Mayer himself, no matter what she might order for lunch or dinner (as legend has it), chicken soup and water were always placed before her with absolutely no substitutions.

With the full power of MGM's makeup, hair, and wardrobe departments behind her, it wouldn't take long for the teenage Judy Garland to mature into a beautiful and often quite glamorous movie star.

The Contract Player

DY GARLAND - Metro Goldwyn-Mayer

The Ingenue

The Star

Collectibles

The Wizard of Oz

For Metro-Goldwyn-Mayer's first major venture into product licensing, its New York based parent company, Loew's Incorporated, established a royalty department specifically designed for movie tie-in merchandise for *The Wizard of Oz*. However, even with its critical acclaim and tremendous promotional campaign, toy manufacturers remained cautious in the beginning with regards to *Oz* and, as a result, only a limited number of products were actually produced in 1939 and 1940. Instead, fueled by the phenomenal merchandising success surrounding Walt Disney's *Snow White and the Seven Dwarfs*, two years earlier, many toy manufacturers placed their money on Walt Disney's up-coming, second animated feature film *Pinocchio*. Several *Oz* products bearing Judy Garland's name or likeness were eventually manufactured for Christmas shoppers in 1939, although they remained somewhat limited in production.

The Wizard of Oz campaign book was distributed to theater owners throughout the country in 1939. Included were illustrations of all poster art, lobby cards, tie-in merchandise, contest suggestions, and instructions on how to exploit, advertise, and publicize the "Wonder Show of Shows." **j.**

Prior to the film's 1939 theatrical release, promotional stationary was created for Loew's Incorporated executives, featuring a special "Wizard of Oz" letterhead with character illustrations drawn by artist Al Hirschfeld. **c.**

The Economy Novelty & Printing Co., of New York, produced a set of five pin-back buttons in 1939. As instructed in the *Oz* campaign book, theater owners were encouraged to use the buttons for lucky number contest purposes or to form a "Wizard of Oz" club with the cooperation of local newspapers. Participants selling a pre-determined amount of new subscriptions would receive a button and a free admission ticket to the film. **c.**

This billboard-size, twenty-four sheet movie poster from the 1939 theatrical release of *Oz* promises audiences "Gaiety! Glory! Glamour!" Measures 9 feet in height x 20 feet in length. **k.**

The original 1939 title card from a set of eight hand-tinted, full color lobby cards. Measures 11 x 14 inches. **k.**

Midget window card, measuring 8 x 14 inches. In original issued condition, the top portion of this 1939 card featured a 4-inch blank border used by motion picture exhibitors to imprint theater name, show dates, times, and location. **j.**

Above: The August 1939 cover of *Movie Life* magazine, featuring Judy Garland as Dorothy. **f.**

Above Right: Judy Garland, Bert Lahr, and Jack Haley, as illustrated by artist Earl Christy for *Screen Romances*, August 1939. **f.**

Above: "The Wizard of Oz Comes to Life." The August 14, 1939, Metro-Goldwyn-Mayer *STUDIO NEWS* magazine, featuring photographs, articles, and insider information regarding the production and promotion of the film. **f.**

Above Right: *Cinémonde* magazine, published in France, September 6, 1939. **f.**

The Ideal Novelty & Toy Co. of Long Island City, New York, entered into negotiations with Loew's Incorporated and its newly formed licensing department in early 1939 for the exclusive rights to produce the very first Judy Garland doll. Made of composition, the doll was available in three sizes. The all original 15-inch doll, shown here with Ideal's cloth doll "The Strawman by Ray Bolger," wears her original wrist tag identifying her as "*Judy Garland* as Dorothy in The Wizard of Oz." Sculpted by artist Bernard Lipfert, the doll was designed in "story book" fashion, bearing little, if any, actual resemblance to Judy Garland. **i.** Dorothy; **j.** Strawman

The Spiegel catalog company featured the "Judy Garland as Dorothy" doll in their Christmas 1939 mail-order ads.

Above: With music and lyrics by Harold Arlen and E.Y. Harburg, six song sheets were issued in 1939 by music publisher Leo Feist, Inc. "Ding-Dong! The Witch Is Dead" and "The Jitterbug" complete the set as shown. Cut from the final print of the MGM motion picture, the song "The Jitterbug" would also eventually be deleted from later printings of the musical selections. **b.** each; **d.** "The Jitterbug"

Above Right: Souvenir Album published by Leo Feist, Inc. in 1940. The illustrated folio contains music and lyrics, plus stills from the MGM motion picture. **c.**

Above: Providing readers with lyrics to the latest popular *Song Hits,* this December 1939 magazine cover featured Judy Garland as Dorothy. **b.**

Above Right: Studio recordings of Judy Garland performing "Over the Rainbow" and "The Jitterbug" are included in this Decca four record, 78 rpm album "presenting the Musical Score from Metro-Goldwyn-Mayer's Motion Picture *Triumph,*" released in the fall of 1939. Other musical selections are performed by the Ken Darby Singers, with Victor Young and His Orchestra. **e.**

"Wizard of Oz Par-T-Masks" were accompanied by a flyer instructing "8 Ways to Have Fun at a Hallowe'en Party." Manufactured by the Einson-Freeman Company, distributed by W.L. Stensgaard & Associates in 1939. **b.** each

Sears, Roebuck & Company offered Christmas 1939 catalog shoppers the opportunity to "Look as cute as Judy Garland!" Manufactured by the L. Gidding Company, this Dorothy-style "Judy Garland dress" was available in age-sizes: 7 to 16. Included with each purchase was an illustrated *Wizard of Oz* story book. **f.**

On July 25, 1956, CBS television announced a deal with MGM for the first nationwide telecast of *The Wizard of Oz*. The motion picture would air on Saturday evening, November 3, 1956, as the finale of the monthly series the *Ford Star Jubilee*. Hosted by Bert Lahr, with a special guest appearance by ten-year-old Liza Minnelli, the program was viewed by more than forty-five million viewers. Within three years, *The Wizard of Oz* became an annual television event and was eventually recognized as the most watched and most beloved film in motion picture history.

By the early 1970s, *The Wizard of Oz* had a worldwide TV audience, and television sponsors and toy manufacturers flooded the market with a variety of Oz related products. In 1989, licensing reached an all time high, in conjunction with the film's 50th Anniversary celebration.

1)   *2)*   *3)*

Contemporary *Oz* collectibles are now widely produced and available in categories ranging from inexpensive items such as plastic drinking glasses and greeting cards to well-crafted, hand-painted porcelain dolls, plates, and figurines. *1)* "Dorothy" from the 1989 series "The Portraits From Oz Plate Collection." Produced by The Hamilton Collection, this porcelain plate features the artwork of artist Thomas Blackshear. **h.** *2)* Cardboard "Dorothy" cut-out figure, designed and produced by Presentation Design Group, Inc. **a.** *3)* Ceramic "Judy Garland as Dorothy" cookie jar, from an *Oz* series produced by Star Jars, 1996. **g+.** *4)* Dorothy costume made exclusively for shoppers at the MGM Grand ® Hotel, Las Vegas, Nevada, 1993. **b.**

4)

Additional *Wizard of Oz* collectibles featuring Judy Garland as Dorothy can be found in the back of the book. See Table 1: *Wizard of Oz* Collectibles (also see chapter on dolls).

Movie Posters & Lobby Cards

As early as 1909, motion picture exhibitors began using posters to promote their up-coming or current attractions. Following World War I, giant motion picture palaces suddenly began springing up all across the country and movie posters, offering only limited listing of film titles and players, quickly grew from their simple beginnings to colorful, hand-painted art forms. Posters would now showcase beautiful portraits of Hollywood's greatest stars, combined with graphically appealing billboard-style advertising. By the mid 1930s, there were several sizes and types of movie posters, each designed for a different display purpose.

Lobby Card
11 x 14 inches. Produced (usually) in sets of eight, consisting of a Title Card displaying the major characters and film title combined with a smaller version of the poster art, along with seven scene cards depicting hand-tinted, color photographs from the motion picture. Printed on heavy stock.

Window Card
22 x 14 inches. Featuring a 4-inch blank border on the top of the card, used to imprint show dates, theater name, and location. Designed to be distributed for use in display windows by local merchants. A much rarer Midget Window Card was also available, 8 x 14 inches. Printed on heavy stock.

Insert
36 x 14 inches. Narrow, vertical poster format. Printed on a slightly heavier paper stock.

Half-Sheet
22 x 28 inches. Often referred to as a Display Card. Produced as simply a larger version of the Lobby "Title" Card. Printed on heavy stock paper.

One-Sheet
41 x 27 inches. Often produced in two versions. The most widely produced and desirable size for collectors. Printed on light paper stock.

Three-Sheet
81 x 41 inches. Roughly twice the size of a One-Sheet. Printed on light paper.

Six-Sheet
81 x 81 inches. Much rarer than the Three-Sheet. Printed on standard paper stock.

Twenty-Four-Sheet
9 x 20 feet. The rarest of all poster sizes, designed to be pasted onto billboards. Printed on paper stock.

Foreign
Depending on the country of origin, foreign posters are often found in varying sizes and paper stocks.

Campaign Book
Also known as a Press Book. Distributed to film exhibitors and theater owners, containing all promotional materials available including: poster art, reviews, biographies, press releases, sample ads, and ideas for contests. Created for the "A" (main attraction/first feature) motion pictures.

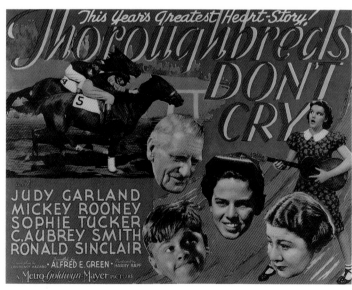

Thoroughbreds Don't Cry, 1937.
Title lobby card, 11 inches x 14 inches. **f.**

Broadway Melody of 1938.
One-sheet, 41 inches x 27 inches. **h.**

Listen Darling, 1938.
Half-sheet, 22 inches x 28 inches. **g.**

Left: *Everybody Sing*, 1938.
One-sheet, 41 inches x 27 inches. **h.**

Above: *Listen Darling*, 1938.
One-sheet, 41 inches x 27 inches. **h.**

Love Finds Andy Hardy, 1938.
Lobby cards, 11 inches x 14 inches. **f.** each

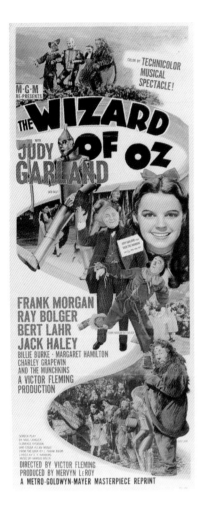

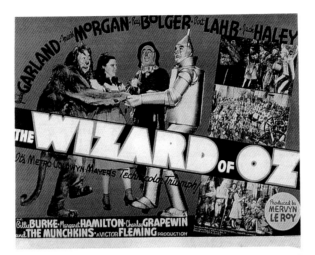

Above Left: *The Wizard of Oz*, 1939.
Insert, for the 1949 re-issue, 36 inches x 14 inches. **i.**

Above Center: *The Wizard of Oz*, 1939.
Two original half-sheets, 22 inches x 28 inches. **k.** each

Above Right: *The Wizard of Oz*, 1939.
Insert, for the 1955 re-issue, 36 inches x 14 inches. **g.**

The Wizard of Oz, 1939.
Two lobby cards, for the 1949 re-issue, 11 inches x 14 inches. **e.** each

The Wizard of Oz, 1939.
One-sheet, for the 1989 Fiftieth Anniversary
re-issue, 41 inches x 27 inches. **c.**

The Wizard of Oz, 1939.
Advertising one-sheet style poster, produced by
the Norman James Company, Ltd., Canada, 1989. **b.**

Babes in Arms, 1939.
Three-sheet, 81 inches x 41 inches. **i.**

Babes in Arms, 1939.
One-sheet, 41 inches x 27 inches. **h.**

Babes in Arms, 1939.
Three-sheet, 81 inches x 41 inches. **i.**

Andy Hardy Meets Debutante, 1940.
Insert, 36 inches x 14 inches. **f.**

Andy Hardy Meets Debutante, 1940.
One-sheet, 41 inches x 27 inches. **g.**

Andy Hardy Meets Debutante, 1940.
Three-sheet, 81 inches x 41 inches. **i.**

Andy Hardy Meets Debutante, 1940.
Six-sheet, 81 inches x 81 inches. **j.**

Andy Hardy Meets Debutante, 1940.
Half-sheet, 22 inches x 28 inches. **f.**

Strike Up the Band, 1940.
One-sheet, 41 inches x 27 inches. **h.**

Strike Up the Band, 1940.
Six-sheet, 81 inches x 81 inches. **j.**

Strike Up the Band, 1940.
Three-sheet, 81 inches x 41 inches. **i.**

Strike Up the Band, 1940.
Half-sheet, 22 inches x 28 inches. **g.**

Strike Up the Band, 1940.
One-sheet, 41 inches x 27 inches. **h.**

Little Nellie Kelly, 1940.
Title lobby card, 11 inches x 14 inches. **f.**

Little Nellie Kelly, 1940.
Title lobby card, 11 inches x 14 inches. **f.**

Little Nellie Kelly, 1940.
One-Sheet, 41 inches x 27 inches. **h.**

Little Nellie Kelly, 1940.
Three-sheet, 81 inches x 41 inches. **j.**

Little Nellie Kelly, 1940.
One-sheet, 41 inches x 27 inches. **h.**

Ziegfeld Girl, 1941.
One-sheet, 41 inches x 27 inches. **i.**

Ziegfeld Girl, 1941.
Three-sheet, 81 inches x 41 inches. **j.**

Ziegfeld Girl, 1941.
Insert, 36 inches x 14 inches. **h.**

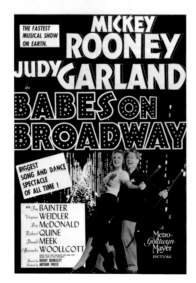

Babes on Broadway, 1941.
Midget window card, 8 inches x 14 inches. **g.**

Babes on Broadway, 1941.
Insert, 36 inches x 14 inches. **g.**

Babes on Broadway, 1941.
Half-sheet, 22 inches x 28 inches. **g.**

Babes on Broadway, 1941.
Six-sheet, 81 inches x 81 inches. **k.**

Babes on Broadway, 1941.
One-sheet, 41 inches x 27 inches. **h.**

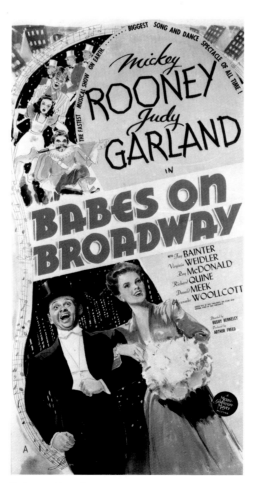

Babes on Broadway, 1941.
Three-sheet, 81 inches x 41 inches. **j.**

Babes on Broadway, 1941.
One-sheet, 41 inches x 27 inches. **h.**

Babes on Broadway, 1941.
Three-sheet, 81 inches x 41 inches. **j.**

For Me and My Gal, 1942.
Midget window card, 8 inches x 14 inches. **g.**

For Me and My Gal, 1942.
Insert, 36 inches x 14 inches. **g.**

For Me and My Gal, 1942.
Half-sheet, 22 inches x 28 inches. **g.**

For Me and My Gal, 1942.
Half-sheet, 22 inches x 28 inches. **g.**

For Me and My Gal, 1942.
Three-sheet, 81 inches x 41 inches. **j.**

For Me and My Gal, 1942.
One-sheet, 41 inches x 27 inches. **h.**

For Me and My Gal, 1942.
One-sheet, 41 inches x 27 inches. **h.**

Presenting Lily Mars, 1943.
Half-sheet, 22 inches x 28 inches. **g.**

Presenting Lily Mars, 1943.
Half-sheet, 22 inches x 28 inches. **f.**

Presenting Lily Mars, 1943.
One-sheet, 41 inches x 27 inches. **h.**

Presenting Lily Mars, 1943.
Three-sheet, 81 inches x 41 inches. **i.**

Presenting Lily Mars, 1943.
Three-sheet, 81 inches x 41 inches. **i.**

Presenting Lily Mars, 1943.
Insert, 36 inches x 14 inches. **f.**

Girl Crazy, 1943.
Title card, 11 inches x 14 inches. **h.**

Girl Crazy, 1943.
One-sheet, 41 inches x 27 inches. **g.**

Thousands Cheer, 1943.
Half-sheet, 22 inches x 28 inches. **f.**

Girl Crazy, 1943.
One-sheet, 41 inches x 27 inches. **g.**

Meet Me in St. Louis, 1944.
Insert, 36 inches x 14 inches. **i.**

Meet Me in St. Louis, 1944.
One-sheet, 41 inches x 27 inches. **i.**

Meet Me in St. Louis, 1944.
Three-sheet, 81 inches x 41 inches. **j.**

Meet Me in St. Louis, 1944.
Half-sheet, 22 inches x 28 inches. **i.**

Meet Me in St. Louis, 1944.
Title lobby card, 11 inches x 14 inches. **h.**

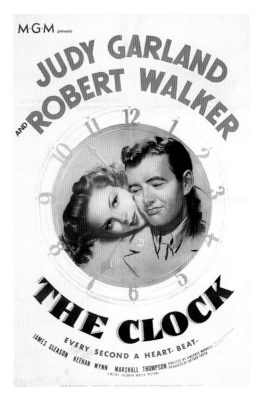

Meet Me in St. Louis, 1944.
Six-sheet, 81 inches x 81 inches. **k.**

The Clock, 1945.
One-sheet, 41 inches x 27 inches. **h.**

The Clock, 1945.
Half-sheet, 22 inches x 28 inches. **g.**

The Harvey Girls, 1946.
Title card with complete set of seven lobby cards, 11 inches x 14 inches.
h. set.

The Harvey Girls, 1946.
Half-sheet, 22 inches x 28 inches. **g.**

The Harvey Girls, 1946.
One-sheet, 41 inches x 27 inches. **h.**

Till the Clouds Roll By, 1946.
One-sheet, 41 inches x 27 inches. **g.**

Ziegfeld Follies, 1946.
Lobby card, 11 inches x 14 inches. **f.**

The Pirate, 1948.
Title card, 11 inches x 14 inches. **g.**

The Pirate, 1948.
One-sheet, 41 inches x 27 inches. **h.**

The Pirate, 1948.
Insert, 36 inches x 14 inches. **g.**

The Pirate, 1948.
Six-sheet, 81 inches x 81 inches. **j.**

Easter Parade, 1948.
One-sheet, 41 inches x 27 inches. **h.**

Easter Parade, 1948.
Three-sheet, 81 inches x 41 inches. **i.**

Easter Parade, 1948.
Title lobby card, 11 inches x 14 inches. **h.**

Easter Parade, 1948.
Two Half-sheets, 22 inches x 28 inches. **g.** each

In the Good Old Summertime, 1949.
Half-sheet, 22 inches x 28 inches. **f.**

In the Good Old Summertime, 1949.
Three-sheet, 81 inches x 41 inches. **h.**

Summer Stock, 1950.
Title card, with complete set of seven lobby
cards, 11 inches x 14 inches. **g. set**

Summer Stock, 1950.
Six-sheet, 81 inches x 81 inches. **i.**

Summer Stock, 1950.
Three Sheet, 81 inches x 41 inches. **h.**

Summer Stock, 1950.
Half-sheet, 22 inches x 28 inches. **f.**

Summer Stock, 1950.
Half-sheet, 22 inches x 28 inches. **f.**

A Star Is Born, 1954.
One-sheet, 41 inches x 27 inches. **h.**

A Star Is Born, 1954.
Australian insert, 36 inches x 14 inches. **f.**

A Star Is Born, 1954.
French, exact size unknown. **h.**

Judgment at Nuremberg, 1961.
Lobby card, 11 inches x 14 inches. **c.**

Gay Purr-ee, 1962.
Set of eight lobby cards, 11 inches x 14 inches.
d. set.

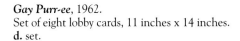

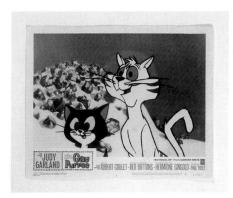

A Child Is Waiting, 1963.
Three lobby cards, 11 inches x 14 inches. **b.** each

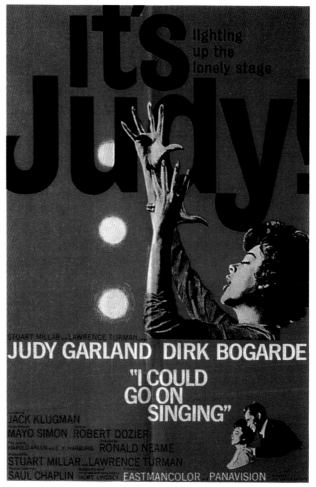

I Could Go On Singing, 1963.
French window-card, 22 inches x 14 inches. **f.**

I Could Go On Singing, 1963.
One-sheet, 41 inches x 27 inches. **e.**

I Could Go On Singing, 1963.
Set of eight lobby cards, 11 inches x 14 inches.
g. set

Advertising & Promotional Art

Advertising strategies using celebrity endorsements provided motion picture studios and product manufacturers with a perfect vehicle in which to capture the public's attention. By the mid 1930s, the entire Hollywood Star System could be found on nearly every conceivable advertising venue, promoting and selling everything from makeup to mink.

The Cover Girl

By the early 1930s, movie magazines had developed into a powerful medium for creating, enhancing, or repairing the public image of Hollywood's most famous personalities. Elaborate photo-spreads, combined with highly embellished articles and biographies, provided readers with an unending supply of information on the career and personal life of their favorite star. But, it was the cover that actually sold the magazine, and few stars graced as many magazine covers throughout the 1930s and 40s as Metro-Goldwyn-Mayer's "girl-next-door"—Judy Garland.

October 29, 1939

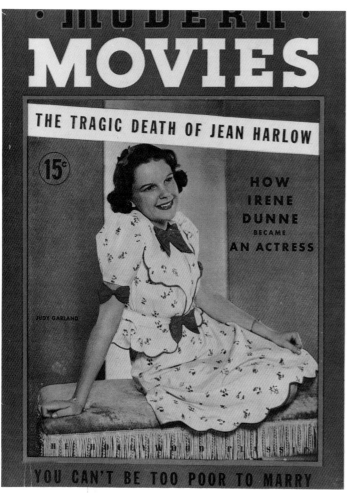

June 1937

February 1939

December 1939

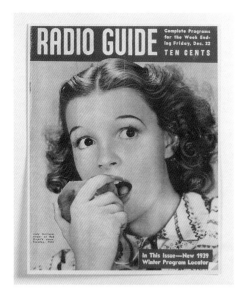

December 22, 1939

January 2, 1940

February 1940

May 7, 1940

September 1940

July 7, 1940

August 1940

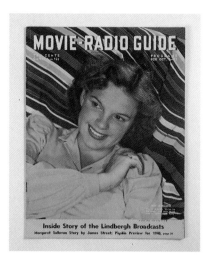

October 1940

October 8, 1940

October 1940

December 1940

March 1941

1941

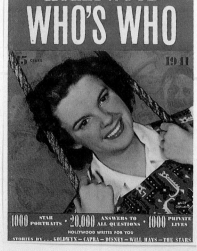

February 1941

April 1941

April 1941

April 19-25, 1941

June 1941

August 1941

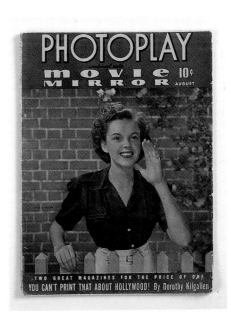

August 1941

August 1941

September 13-19, 1941

October 1941

January 1942

February 1942

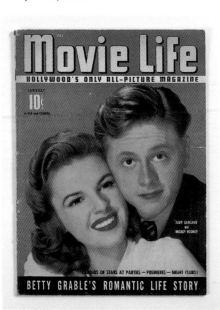

January 1942

July 1942

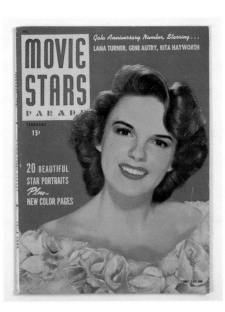

February 1943

April 1943

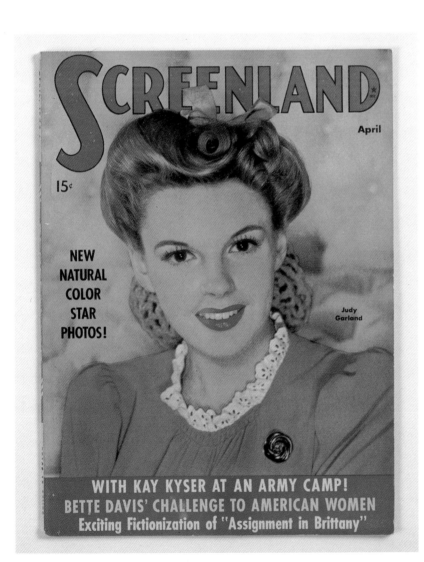

April 1943

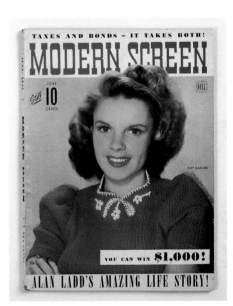

June 1943

July 1943

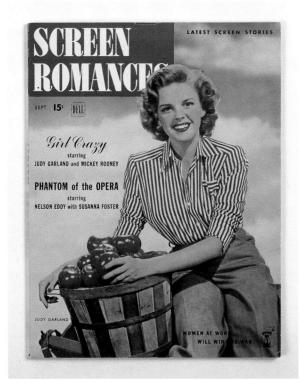

September 1943

Fall 1943

December 1943

Summer 1944

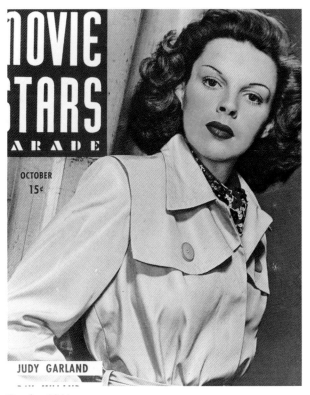

October 1944

November 1944

November 1944

December 1944

November 1945

December 1945

December 1945

November 1945

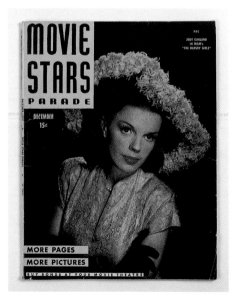

December 1945

February 1946

March 1946

May 1948

August 1948

August 1948

October 1948

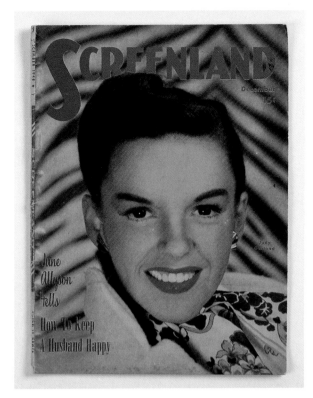

December 1948

January 1949

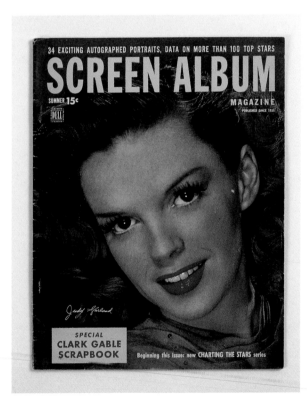

Summer 1949

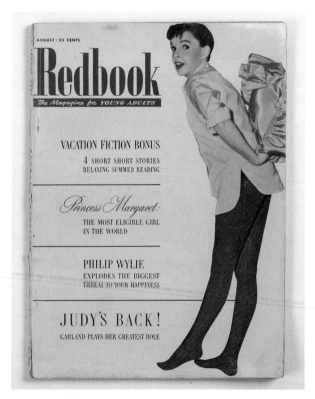

August 1954

January 1955

January 1955

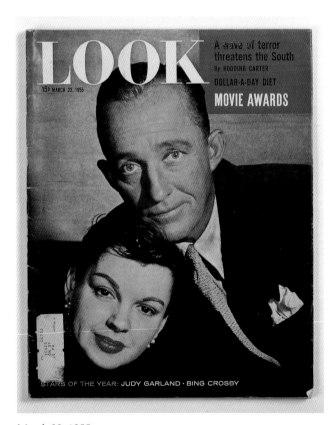

March 22, 1955

March 27, 1955

April 10, 1962

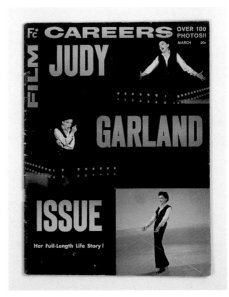

March 1963

October 1963

October 31, 1961

May 18, 1964

1971

Sweden, August 13, 1939

France, September 1939

Spain, 1941

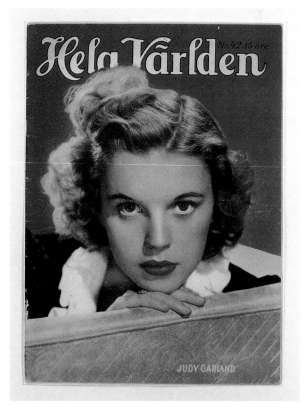

Sweden, 1940

Denmark, July 1944

Argentina, August 1941

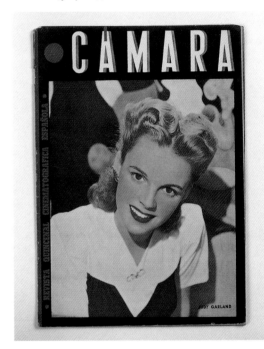

Spain, October 1945

Norway, December 1944

France, November 30, 1945

France, April 1946

France, July 1948

Italy, 1948

France, April 20, 1955

France, November 1961

Sheet Music

Judy Garland's extraordinary vocal abilities and remarkable sense of timing and pitch were showcased throughout her career in a repeated formula that arranged the key and tempo of her songs so that it seemed she would never be able to reach the last note. This way there was always cheering when she did! With the enormous popularity of her MGM musicals and her successful recording contract with Decca records, composers and lyricists were quick to realize that if Judy Garland sang your song, you were guaranteed a hit.

"You Made Me Love You (I didn't want to do it)," from *Broadway Melody of 1938*. Music and Lyrics by James V. Monaco & Joe McCarthy, © 1913 by Broadway Music Corporation.

"It's Love I'm After," from *Pigskin Parade*. Music and Lyrics by Lew Pollack & Sidney D. Mitchell, © 1936 by Movietone Music Corp. Sole Selling Agents Sam Fox Publishing Company. Additional songs published from this 20th Century-Fox motion picture include: "Balboa," "You Do the Darndest Things Baby," and "You're Slightly Terrific."

"Everybody Sing," from *Broadway Melody of 1938*. Music and Lyrics by Nacio Herb Brown & Arthur Freed, © 1937 by Robbins Music Corporation. Additional songs published from this MGM motion picture include: "Follow in My Footsteps," "I'm Feeling Like a Million," "Your Broadway and My Broadway," and "Yours and Mine."

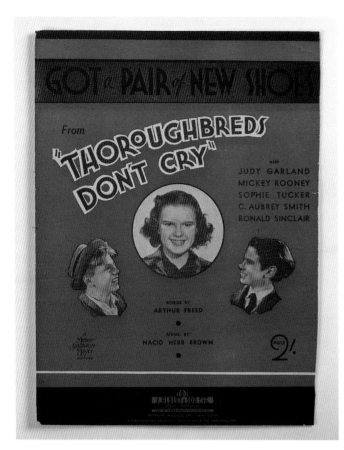

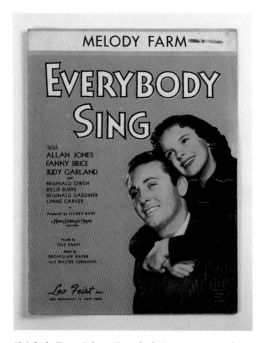

"Melody Farm," from *Everybody Sing*. Music and Lyrics by Brownislaw Kaper, Walter Jurmann & Gus Kahn, © 1937 by Leo Feist, Inc. Additional songs published from this MGM motion picture include: "Swing Mr. Mendelssohn," "The One I Love," and "Quainty Dainty Me."

"Got a Pair of New Shoes," from *Thoroughbreds Don't Cry*. Music and Lyrics by Nacio Herb Brown & Arthur Freed, © 1937 by Robbins Music Corporation and by J. Albert & Son Pty. Ltd., Sidney, Australia (as shown).

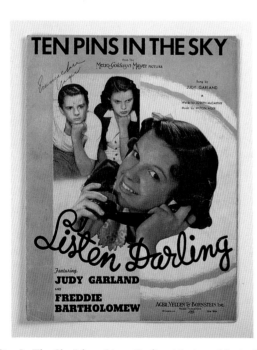

"Ten Pins In The Sky," from *Listen Darling*. Music and Lyrics by Milton Ager & Joseph McCarthy, © 1938 by Ager, Yellen & Bornstein, Inc. Additional songs published from this MGM motion picture include: "Zing! Went the Strings of My Heart" and "On The Bumpy Road to Love."

"Nine Pins In The Sky," from *Listen Darling*. Music and Lyrics by Milton Ager & Joseph McCarthy, © 1938 by Ager, Yellen & Bornstein, Inc. and by The Sun Music Publishing Co., Ltd., London, England (as shown). **c.**

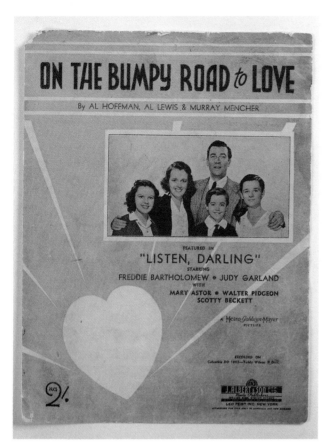

"In-Between," from *Love Finds Andy Hardy*. Music and Lyrics by Roger Edens, © 1938 by Leo Feist Inc. Additional songs published from this MGM motion picture include: "It Never Rains, But What It Pours" and "Meet The Beat Of My Heart."

"On The Bumpy Road to Love," from *Listen Darling*. Music and Lyrics by Al Hoffman, Al Lewis & Murray Mencher, © 1938 by Leo Feist Inc. and by J. Albert & Son Pty. Ltd., Sidney, Australia (as shown).

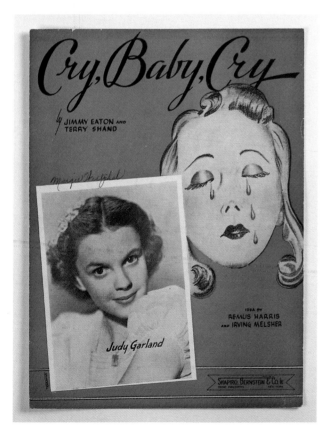

"Meet The Beat Of My Heart," from *Love Finds Andy Hardy*. Music and Lyrics by Harry Revel & Mack Gordon, © 1938 by Leo Feist, Inc. and by J. Albert & Son Pty. Ltd., Sidney, Australia (as shown).

"Cry, Baby, Cry," from the Decca recording #1796. Music and Lyrics by Jimmy Eaton & Terry Shand, © 1938 by The Peter Maurice Music Co. Sole Selling Agents Shapiro, Bernstein & Co.

"Over The Rainbow" and "We're Off To See The Wizard" from *The Wizard of Oz*. Music and Lyrics by Harold Arlen & E.Y. Harburg, © 1939 by Leo Feist, Inc. and by Francis, Day & Hunter Ltd., London, England (as shown). Additional songs published from this MGM motion picture include: "Ding-Dong! The Witch is Dead," "If I Only Had a Brain," "The Jitterbug," and "The Merry Old Land of Oz." **c.** each

"Good Morning," from *Babes in Arms*. Music and Lyrics by Nacio Herb Brown & Arthur Freed, © 1939 by Loew's Incorporated and by Chappell & Co., Inc., London, England (as shown). Additional songs published from this MGM motion picture include: "Babes in Arms," "God's Country," "I Cried For You," "I'm Just Wild About Harry," and "Where or When."

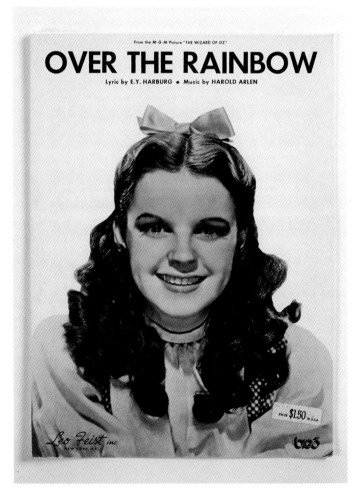

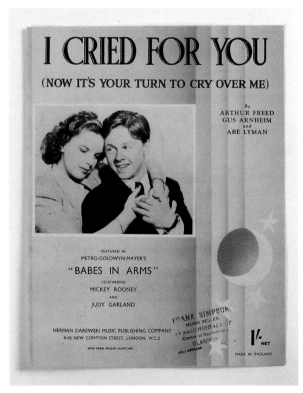

"Over The Rainbow," from *The Wizard Of Oz*. Music and Lyrics by Harold Arlen & E.Y. Harburg, © 1939 by Leo Feist, Inc., reissued cover ©1967.

"I Cried For You (Now It's Your Turn To Cry Over Me)," from *Babes in Arms*. Music and Lyrics by Arthur Freed, Gus Arnheim & Abe Lyman, © 1923 by Sherman, Clay & Co. and by Herman Darewski Music Publishing Co., London, England (as shown).

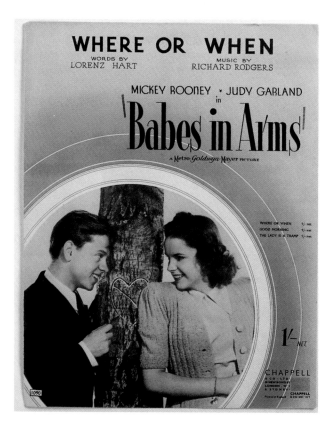

"Where or When," from *Babes in Arms*. Music and Lyrics by Richard Rodgers & Lorenz Hart, © 1937 by Chappell & Co., Inc., London, England (as shown).

"Our Love Affair," from *Strike Up the Band*. Music and Lyrics by Roger Edens & Arthur Freed, © 1940 by Leo Feist, Inc. Additional songs published from this MGM motion picture include: "Drummer Boy," "Nobody," and "Strike Up the Band."

"Our Love Affair," from *Strike Up the Band*. Music and Lyrics by Roger Edens & Arthur Freed, © 1940 by Leo Feist, Inc. and by Francis, Day & Hunter Ltd., London, England (as shown).

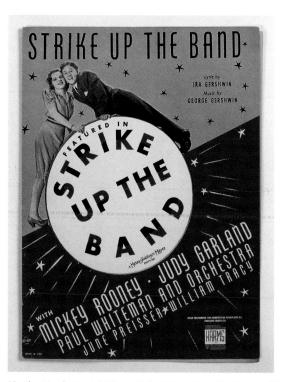

"Strike Up the Band," from *Strike Up the Band*. Music and Lyrics by George & Ira Gershwin, © 1940 by New World Music Corporation, Sole Selling Agent Harms Inc.

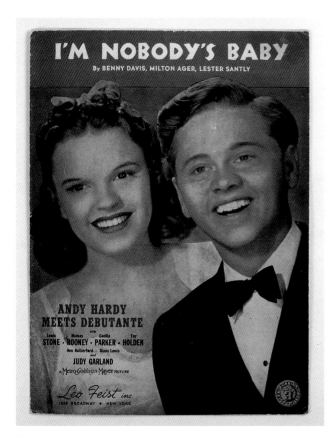

"I'm Nobody's Baby," from *Andy Hardy Meets Debutante*. Music and Lyrics by Benny Davis, Milton Ager & Lester Santly, © 1921 by Leo Feist, Inc. Additional songs published from this MGM motion picture include: "Alone" and "Buds Won't Bud."

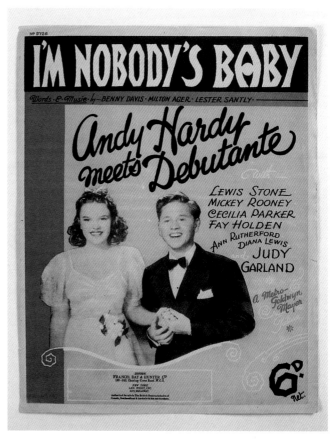

"I'm Nobody's Baby," from *Andy Hardy Meets Debutante*. Music and Lyrics by Benny Davis, Milton Ager & Lester Santly, © 1921 by Leo Feist, Inc. and by Francis, Day & Hunter Ltd., London, England (as shown).

"A Pretty Girl Milking Her Cow," from *Little Nellie Kelly*. Music and Lyrics Adaptation by Roger Edens, © 1940 by Leo Feist, Inc. and by J. Albert & Son Pty. Ltd., Sidney, Australia (as shown).

"It's a Great Day for the Irish," from *Little Nellie Kelly*. Music and Lyrics by Roger Edens, © 1940 by Leo Feist, Inc. and by J. Albert & Son Pty. Ltd., Sidney, Australia (as shown in green). Additional songs published from this MGM motion picture include: "Nellie Kelly I Love You," "A Pretty Girl Milking Her Cow," and "Singin' in the Rain."

Above: "Nellie Kelly I Love You," from *Little Nellie Kelly*. Music and Lyrics by George M. Cohan, © 1922 by M. Whitmark & Sons and by J. Albert & Son Pty. Ltd., Sidney, Australia (as shown).

Above Center: "Nellie Kelly I Love You," from *Little Nellie Kelly*. Music and Lyrics by George M. Cohan, © 1922 by M. Whitmark & Sons.

Above Right: "Minnie From Trinidad," from *Ziegfeld Girl*. Music and Lyrics by Roger Edens, © 1941 by Leo Feist, Inc. Additional songs published from this MGM motion picture include: "Caribbean Love Song," "I'm Always Chasing Rainbows," "Mister Gallagher and Mister Shean," "You Stepped Out of a Dream," and "We Must Have Music."

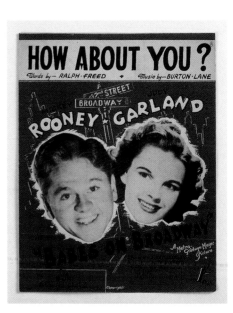

Above: "Chin Up! Cheerio! Carry On!" from *Babes on Broadway*. Music and Lyrics by Burton Lane & Ralph Freed, © 1941 by Leo Feist, Inc. Additional songs published from this MGM motion picture include: "Hoe Down," "How About You?" and "Waiting for the Robert E. Lee."

Above Center: "Waiting for the Robert E. Lee," from *Babes on Broadway*. Music and Lyrics by L. Wolfe Gilbert & Lewis F. Muir, © 1912 by F. A. Mills. Copyright renewed and assigned 1940 to Alfred Music Co.

Above Right: "How About You?" from *Babes on Broadway*. Music and Lyrics by Burton Lane & Ralph Freed, © 1941 by Leo Feist, Inc. and by The Sun Publishing Co., Ltd., London, England (as shown).

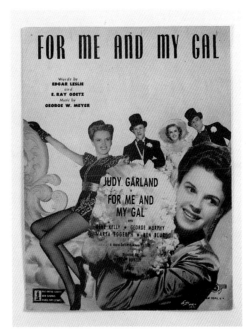

Above: "Chin Up! Cheerio! Carry On!," from *Babes on Broadway*. Music and Lyrics by Burton Lane & E.Y. Harburg, © 1941 by Leo Feist, Inc. and by J. Albert & Son Pty. Ltd., Sidney, Australia (as shown).

Above Center: "For Me and My Gal," from *For Me and My Gal*. Music and Lyrics by George W. Meyer & Edgar Leslie and E. Ray Goetz, © 1917 by Waterson, Berlin & Snyder Co., Canada (as shown).

Above Right: "For Me and My Gal," from *For Me and My Gal*. Music and Lyrics by George W. Meyer & Edgar Leslie and E. Ray Goetz, © 1917 by Waterson, Berlin & Snyder Co. Copyright assigned 1932 to Mills Music, Inc. Additional songs published from this MGM motion picture include: "After You've Gone," "How 'Ya Gonna Keep 'Em Down on the Farm?" "They Go Wild, Simply Wild Over Me," and "When You Wore a Tulip and I Wore a Big Red Rose."

Above: "When You Wore a Tulip and I Wore a Big Red Rose," from *For Me and My Gal*. Music and Lyrics by Percy Wenrich & Jack Mahoney, © 1914 by Leo Feist, Inc. and by Aschberg, Hopwood & Crew, Ltd., London, England (as shown).

Above Center: "When I Look at You," from *Presenting Lily Mars*. Music and Lyrics by Walter Jurmann & Paul Francis Webster, © 1926 by Leo Feist, Inc. Additional songs published from this MGM motion picture include: "Broadway Rhythm," "Every Little Movement," and "Is It Really Love?"

Above Right: "When I Look at You," from *Presenting Lily Mars*. Music and Lyrics by Walter Jurmann & Paul Francis Webster, © 1926 by Leo Feist, Inc. and by The Sun Publishing Co. Ltd., London, England (as shown).

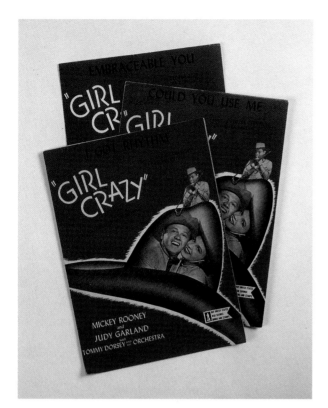

"I Got Rhythm," from *Girl Crazy.* Music and Lyrics by George & Ira Gershwin, © 1930 by New World Music Corp. Sole Selling Agent Harms Inc. Additional songs published from this MGM motion picture include: "Bidin' My Time," "But Not For Me," "Could You Use Me?" "Embraceable You," and "Treat Me Rough."

"Bidin' My Time," from *Girl Crazy.* Music and Lyrics by George and Ira Gershwin, © 1930 by New World Music Corp. Sole Selling Agent Harms Inc., also published by Chappell & Co., Ltd., London, England (as shown).

"The Joint Is Really Jumpin' in Carnegie Hall," from *Thousands Cheer.* Music and Lyrics by Roger Edens, Ralph Blaine & Hugh Martin, © 1943 by Leo Feist, Inc. Additional songs published from this MGM motion picture include: "Honeysuckle Rose," "I Dug a Ditch," "Let There Be Music," "Three Letters in the Mailbox," "United Nations on the March," and "Daybreak."

"The Joint Is Really Jumpin' in Carnegie Hall," from *Thousands Cheer.* Music and Lyrics by Roger Edens, Ralph Blaine & Hugh Martin, © 1943 by Leo Feist, Inc. and by J. Albert & Son Pty. Ltd., Sidney, Australia (as shown).

"Meet Me in St. Louis, Louis," from *Meet Me in St. Louis.* Music and Lyrics by Kerry Mills & Andrew B. Sterling, © 1904 by F. A. Mills. Copyright assigned 1935 to Jerry Vogel Music Co.

"The Boy Next Door," from *Meet Me in St. Louis.* Music and Lyrics by Ralph Blane & Hugh Martin, © 1944 by Leo Feist, Inc. Additional songs published from this MGM motion picture include: "The Trolley Song," "Have Yourself a Merry Little Christmas," "Skip to My Lou," "Under the Bamboo Tree," and "You and I."

"Under the Bamboo Tree," from *Meet Me in St. Louis.* Music and Lyrics by Bob Cole, © 1902 by Jos. W. Stern & Co. Copyright assigned 1932 to Edward B. Marks Music Corporation.

"Meet Me in St. Louis, Louis," from *Meet Me in St. Louis.* Music and Lyrics by Kerry Mills & Andrew B. Sterling, © 1904 by F. A. Mills. Copyright assigned 1928 to Paull-Pioneer Music Co., also published by Canadian Music Sales Corporation Ltd., Toronto, Canada (as shown).

Above: "The Boy Next Door," from *Meet Me in St. Louis*. Music and Lyrics by Ralph Blane & Hugh Martin, © 1944 by Leo Feist, Inc. and by The Sun Music Publishing Co. Ltd., London, England (as shown).

Above Center: "The Trolley Song/La Chanson du Trolley," from *Meet Me in St. Louis*. Music and Lyrics by Ralph Blane & Hugh Martin, © 1944 by Leo Feist, Inc. and by Editions France-Mélodie, Paris, France (as shown). c.

Above Right: "The Trolley Song," from *Meet Me in St. Louis*. Music and Lyrics by Ralph Blane & Hugh Martin, © 1944 by Leo Feist, Inc. and by J. Albert & Son Pty. Ltd., Sidney, Australia (as shown).

Above: "On the Atchison, Topeka and the Santa Fe" and "Wait and See," from *The Harvey Girls*. Music and Lyrics by Harry Warren & Johnny Mercer, © 1945 by Leo Feist, Inc. Additional songs published from this MGM motion picture include: "In the Valley (Where the Evenin' Sun Goes Down)," "It's a Great Big World," "My Intuition," "Oh You Kid," "March of the Doagies," "Swing Your Partner Round and Round," "The Train Must Be Fed," and "The Wild, Wild West."

Above Center: "On the Atchison, Topeka and the Santa Fe/Le petit train du Far-West," from *The Harvey Girls*. Music and Lyrics by Harry Warren & Johnny Mercer, © 1945 by Leo Feist, Inc. and by Editions France-Mélodie, Paris, France (as shown). c.

Above Right: "Swing Your Partner Round and Round," from *The Harvey Girls*. Music and Lyrics by Harry Warren & Johnny Mercer, © 1945 by Leo Feist, Inc. and by J. Albert & Son Pty. Ltd., Sidney, Australia (as shown).

Above: "Look for the Silver Lining," from *Till the Clouds Roll By*. Music and Lyrics by Jerome Kern & Bud De Sylva, © 1920 by T. B. Harms Co. Additional songs published from this MGM motion picture include: "All the Things You Are," "Can't Help Lovin' Dat Man," "How'd You Like to Spoon With Me?" "I Won't Dance," "The Land Where Good Songs Go," "The Last Time I Saw Paris," "Ol' Man River," "She Didn't Say Yes," "Smoke Gets in Your Eyes," "They Didn't Believe Me," "Till the Clouds Roll By," "Who?" "Why Was I Born?" and "Yesterdays."

Above Center: "The Last Time I Saw Paris." Music and Lyrics by Jerome Kern & Oscar Hammerstein II, © 1940 by T. B. Harms Company.

Above Right: "There Is No Breeze," from the Decca recording #23746. Music and Lyrics by Alstone & Dorothy Dick, © 1945 by Editions Salabert. Rights controlled by Robbins Music Corporation.

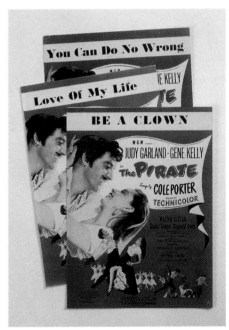

Above: "Connecticut," from the Decca recording #23804. Music and Lyrics by Ralph Blane & Hugh Martin, © 1946 by Harry Warren Music, Inc.

Above Center: "Don't Bite The Hand That's Feeding You." Music and Lyrics by Jimmie Morgan & Thomas Hoier, © 1915 by Leo Feist, Inc.

Above Right: "Be A Clown," from *The Pirate*. Music and Lyrics by Cole Porter, © 1948 by Chappell & Co. Sole Selling Agent T. B. Harms Company. Additional songs published from this MGM motion picture include: "Love of My Life," "Mack the Black," "Nina," and "You Can Do No Wrong."

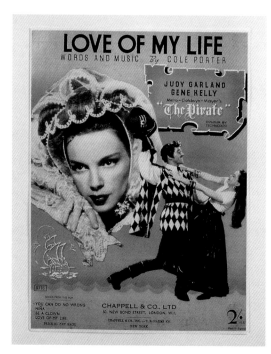

"Love of My Life," from *The Pirate*. Music and Lyrics by Cole Porter, © 1948 by Chappell & Co., Inc., London, England (as shown).

"A Fella With an Umbrella," from *Easter Parade*. Music and Lyrics by Irving Berlin, © 1947 by Irving Berlin Ltd., London, England (as shown).

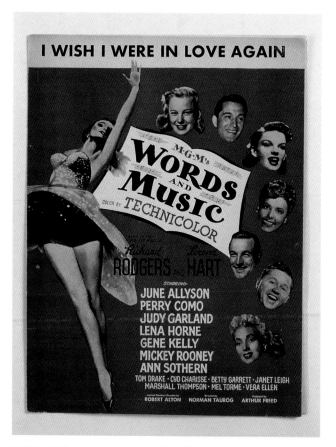

"A Couple of Swells," from *Easter Parade*. Music and Lyrics by Irving Berlin, © 1947 by Irving Berlin Music Corporation. Additional songs published from this MGM motion picture include: "Beautiful Faces," "Better Luck Next Time," "Drum Crazy," "Easter Parade," "Everybody's Doin' It," "A Fella With an Umbrella," "The Girl on the Magazine Cover," "Happy Easter," "I Love Piano," "I Want to Go Back to Michigan," "It Only Happens When I Dance With You," "Mr. Monotony," "Ragtime Violin," "Shakin' the Blues Away," "Snooky Ookums," "Steppin' Out With My Baby," and "When the Midnight Choo Choo Leaves for Alabam."

"I Wish I Were in Love Again," from *Words and Music*. Music and Lyrics by Richard Rodgers & Lorenz Hart, © 1937 by Chappell & Co. Additional songs published from this MGM motion picture include: "Blue Moon," "Blue Room," "Johnny One Note," "The Lady is a Tramp," "Manhattan," "Mountain Greenery," "There's a Small Hotel," "This Can't Be Love," "Thou Swell," "Where or When," "Where's That Rainbow?" and "With a Song in My Heart."

"In the Good Old Summertime," from *In the Good Old Summertime*. Music and Lyrics by George Evans & Ren Shields, © 1902 by Howley, Haviland & Dresser. Copyright assigned 1932 to Edward B. Marks Music Corporation. Additional songs published from this MGM motion picture include: "I Don't Care," "Last Night When We Were Young," "Meet Me Tonight in Dreamland," "Merry Christmas," "Play That Barber Shop Chord," and "Put Your Arms Around Me Honey."

"Put Your Arms Around Me Honey," from *In the Good Old Summertime*. Music and Lyrics by Albert Von Tilzer & Junie McCree, © 1905 by York Music Co. Copyright renewed 1937 by Broadway Music Corp.

"Merry Christmas," from *In the Good Old Summertime*. Music and Lyrics by Fred Spielman & Janice Torre, © 1948 by Loew's Incorporated. Rights throughout the world controlled by Robbins Music Corporation.

"Friendly Star," from *Summer Stock*. Music and Lyrics by Harry Warren & Mack Gordon, © 1950 by Harry Warren Music, Inc. Sole Selling and Licensing Rights controlled by Leo Feist, Inc. Additional songs published from this MGM motion picture include: "Dig, Dig, Dig For Your Dinner," "Get Happy," "(Howdy Neighbor) Happy Harvest," "If You Feel Like Singing, Sing," "Mem'ry Island," and "You Wonderful You."

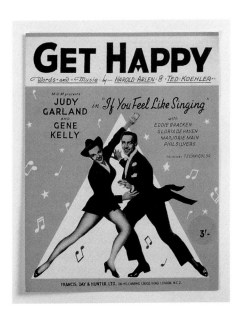

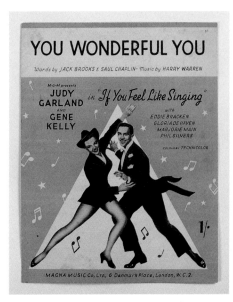

Above: "Get Happy," from *Summer Stock/If You Feel Like Singing* (British title). Music and Lyrics by Harold Arlen & Ted Koehler, © 1930 by Remick Music Corp. and by Francis, Day & Hunter Ltd., London, England (as shown).

Above Center: "Get Happy," from *Summer Stock*. Music and Lyrics by Harold Arlen & Ted Koehler, © 1930 by Remick Music Corp.

Above Right: "You Wonderful You," from *Summer Stock/If You Feel Like Singing* (British title). Music and Lyrics by Harry Warren & Jack Brooks and Saul Chaplin, © 1950 by Harry Warren Music, Inc. and by Magna Music Co., Ltd., London, England (as shown).

Above: "Heartbroken," from the Columbia recording #40023. Music and Lyrics by Phil Springer and Fred Ebb, © 1953 by Redd Evans Music Co. Inc.

Above Center: "Beautiful Trouble" and "That's All There Is (There Isn't Any More)," from *The Letter*, Capital recording #TAO-1188. Music and Lyrics by Gordon Jenkins, © 1959 by Gordon Jenkins Music Corp.

Above Right: "The Man That Got Away," from *A Star Is Born*. Music and Lyrics by Harold Arlen & Ira Gershwin, © 1954 by Harwin Music Corp. Sole Selling Agent Edwin H. Morris & Company. Additional songs published from this Warner Bros. motion picture include: "Gotta Have Me Go With You," "It's A New World," "Lose That Long Face," "The Peanut Vendor," "Swanee," "Born in a Trunk," "Here's What I'm Here For," and "Someone at Last."

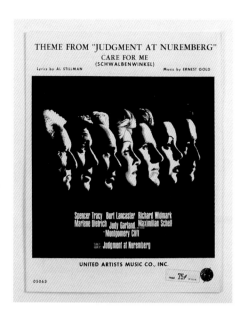

Above: "Theme From *Judgment at Nuremberg*," from *Judgment at Nuremberg*. Music and Lyrics by Ernest Gold & Al Stillman, © 1962 by United Artists Music Co., Inc.

Above Center: "Snowflakes," from *A Child is Waiting*. Music and Lyrics by Marjorie Kurtz, © 1951 by Lombardo Music, Inc.

Above Right: "Little Drops of Rain," from *Gay Purr-ee*. Music and Lyrics by Harold Arlen & E.Y. Harburg, © 1962 by Harwin Music Corporation. Additional songs published from this Warner Bros. animated motion picture include: "Mewsette," "The Money Cat," "Paris Is a Lonely Town," and "Roses Red, Violets Blue."

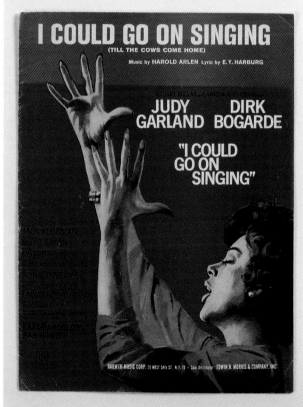

"I Could Go On Singing," from *I Could Go On Singing*. Music and Lyrics by Harold Arlen & E.Y. Harburg, © 1962 by Harwin Music Corporation. Additional songs published from this United Artists motion picture include: "By Myself" and "Hello, Bluebird."

"I'd Like To Hate Myself in the Morning." Music and Lyrics by John Meyer, © 1969 by Arcola Music Inc. Sole Selling Agent Criterion Music Corporation.

Judy Garland was a regular feature on the covers of *Song Hits, Songs,* and *Hit Parader* magazines throughout the 1940s. Published by Charlton Publishing Corporation and Song Lyrics Inc., the magazines featured the printed lyrics to the latest hit songs. **a.** each; Oz cover **c.**

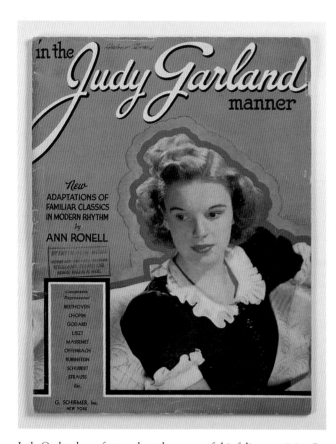

Judy Garland was featured on the cover of this folio containing "new adaptations of familiar classics." Published by G. Schirmer Inc., ©1940. **b.**

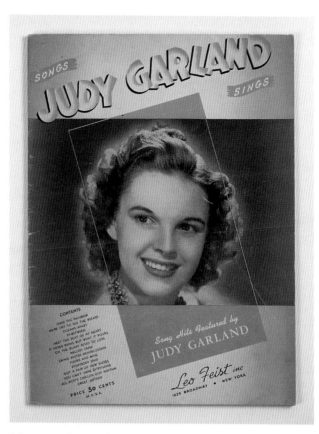

Fifteen song hits are featured in this collection of Judy Garland related music and lyrics. Folio published by Leo Feist, Inc., ©1941. **c.**

The music of George and Ira Gershwin is featured in this folio published by New World Music Corp., ©1954. **b.**

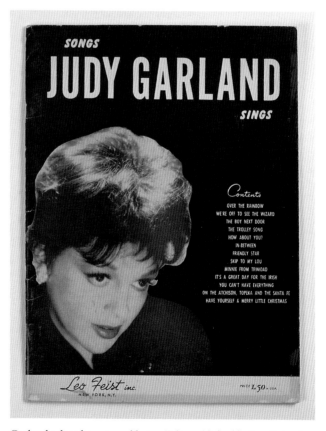

Garland related music and lyrics. Folio published by Leo Feist, Inc., ©1967. **b.**

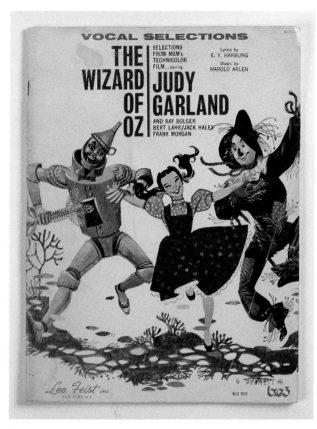

Illustrated folio featuring stills from the MGM motion picture. Folio contains music and lyrics published by Leo Feist, Inc. ©1968. **b.**

Comprehensive collection of Garland related music and lyrics. Illustrated folio published by Chappell & Co., Inc. ©1975. Cover adapted from Judith Woracek Berry's original design. **b.**

This illustrated folio contains music and lyrics from *A Star Is Born*, with exclusive photographs from the restored version of the motion picture. Published by Warner Bros. Publications Inc., ©1983. **b.**

Dolls

Celebrity dolls made in the image of Hollywood's most famous child stars began making their way into the arms of adoring young moviegoers by the early 1920s. Made from a variety of materials such as porcelain, composition, cloth, and paper, dolls made in the image of Jackie Coogan, Baby Peggy, and the cast of the *Our Gang* comedies suddenly allowed children the opportunity to take their favorite little star home with them. Popular celebrity doll lines in the 1930s and 40s included Shirley Temple, Deanna Durbin, the Dionne Quintuplets, and Judy Garland.

This all original, 18-inch composition "Dorothy" doll features large expressive brown eyes, with real and painted lashes and a deep blush found on cheeks, wrists, and knees. Marked on the back of the head "IDEAL DOLL," body is marked "18//IDEAL DOLL//MADE IN USA." An exceptional, mint condition example of this extrememly rare celebrity doll. **i. +**

Manufactured in 1939 by the Ideal Novelty & Toy Co., the "Judy Garland as Dorothy" doll from *The Wizard of Oz* was available in three sizes: 18 inches, 15 inches, and 13 inches. Made of composition, on a fully-jointed six-piece body, the dolls have human hair wigs in varying styles and are costumed in a blue and white gingham dress made of organdy and rayon. Dress is tagged only to indicate size and is a near perfect copy of the original MGM motion picture costume designed by Gilbert Adrian, with only slight variations on the collar and sleeves. The 13-inch doll (the smallest of the three) features a dimple in her chin and has proportionately smaller size eyes than the two larger dolls. **i.** each

The original wrist tag for Ideal's composition "Dorothy" doll. Reverse side of the tag features artwork for Ideal's cloth doll "The Strawman by Ray Bolger of The Wizard of Oz." **c.**

Spiegel catalog of Chicago, Illinois, offered two sizes of the "Judy Garland Dorothy" doll for Christmas 1939. Original prices were listed at $2.79 and $4.69.

This 13-inch composition "Dorothy" doll features an all original outfit made of cotton, reminiscent of W. W. Denslow's original *Oz* illustrations. **i.**

It is uncertain whether or not these two unmarked cloth dolls, circa 1940, are intended to represent "Judy Garland as Dorothy." They are, however, worth noting. Dolls and original clothing appear to be factory made. 25 inches in height. **e.** each

Ideal offered their second "Judy Garland" doll in 1940. Sculpted by Bernard Lipfert, the doll was designed in the style of the company's successful Deanna Durbin doll line. Made of composition, on a fully-jointed six-piece body measuring 21 inches tall, the doll is marked "MADE IN U.S.A." on the back of the head; body is marked "IDEAL DOLL" over a backwards "21." Dolls are dressed in a replica of Judy Garland's MGM costume, originally designed by Dolly Tree for the finale of the motion picture *Strike Up the Band*. Tagged only to indicate size, the floral print organdy gown was available in pink, blue, or white. Pinned to the bodice of each dress is a white portrait pin that reads "JUDY GARLAND DOLL//A METRO GOLDWYN MAYER STAR." Each doll came gifted boxed along with a photograph and autograph facsimile of the star. **h.**

Close-up illustrating the beautiful facial molding of the 21-inch composition "Judy Garland" doll. Human hair wigs were available in varying shades of a deep rich auburn, in a relaxed 1940s style, or with tight pin curls framing the face and shoulders (as shown). Featuring brown sleep eyes made of celluloid, which close when the doll is reclined, with real and painted lashes and dark eye shadow. **h.**

Original heart-shaped wrist tag for the composition "Judy Garland" doll. **c.**

To "MAKE HER CHRISTMAS WISH COME TRUE," Spiegel offered its 1940 Christmas catalog shoppers two sizes of the "grown up and dressed for romance" "Judy Garland" doll. The 18-inch doll was available exclusively by Spiegel on an extremely limited basis.

Above Left: The Mego Toy Corporation created a set of six 8-inch vinyl *Wizard of Oz* dolls in 1975. "Dorothy," authentically costumed from the MGM motion picture, came gift boxed with her basket and dog Toto. **b.**

Above Right: "Judy Garland as Hannah Brown" from *Easter Parade*. Sculpted by Jim Hughes, for World Doll Design Group. Vinyl doll measures 18 inches tall, limited edition of 17,500. 1975. **e.**

For providing the *Los Angeles Examiner* with 2 new subscribers, a "GENUINE 21-INCH JUDY GARLAND doll" was yours free.

Made in England by Peggy Nisbet, 1980. Wrist tag identifies this doll as "Judy Garland in *Meet Me in St. Louis*." 8 inches in height. **d.**

Limited edition, full-body porcelain "Judy Garland as Dorothy." Created in 1983, by doll artist Susan LaChasse. Measures 14 inches in height, with paper-weight glass eyes and human hair wig. Doll is unmarked. **g.**

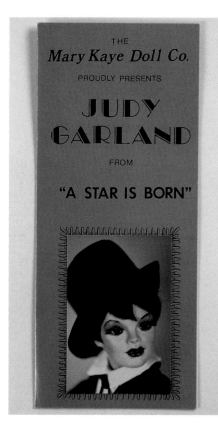

Above: From her role as Vicki Lester in *A Star Is Born,* costumed from the "Born in a Trunk" sequence, this 16-inch full-body porcelain doll was sculpted by Hal Reed for the Mary Kaye Doll Company. Limited edition, marked on the back of the head "JUDY GARLAND//BORN IN A TRUNK//MARY KAYE//HAL REED//1983 MARY KAYE DOLL CO." **g.**

Above Center: The Franklin Mint produced this hand-painted porcelain and cloth "Judy Garland as Dorothy" doll in 1986. First in the series of an entire line of *Oz* dolls, she stands 17 inches tall. Wicker basket with plush Toto included. A custom Emerald City doll stand was available in 1990. **d.**

Above Right: "Judy Garland as Dorothy." Sixth in the "Legend Series" doll line manufactured by Effanbee in 1984. Doll measures 14 ½ inches in height. Made of vinyl. **d.**

The fiftieth anniversary of *The Wizard of Oz,* in 1989, inspired this vinyl and cloth "Judy Garland as Dorothy" doll. Sold with an inter-connecting Yellow Brick Road doll stand that joins the doll with the other characters in the *Oz* series. Manufactured by Presents of California, a division of Hamilton Gifts. 14 inches in height. **b.**

´Using the same facial mold, Presents of California also offered their vinyl "Dorothy" doll in hand puppet form. **b.**

The Madame Alexander Doll Company introduced an 8-inch hard-plastic "Dorothy" doll in 1991, as a part of the "Storyland Doll" series. **c.**

"Barbie ® as Dorothy from *The Wizard of Oz.*" From the Hollywood Legends Collection by Mattel, ™ Inc. 1997. **e.**

Designed exclusively for the Warner Bros. Studio Store in 1998, "Judy Garland as Dorothy" from *The Wizard of Oz.* This unique bean-bag style cloth doll measures 11 inches in height, with embroidered facial features, molded corduroy fabric hair with silk ribbins. **a.**

Illustrated by Queen Holden, the Whitman Publishing Company, Racine, Wisconsin, offered this *Judy Garland Cut-Out Book*, in 1940. An extensive wardrobe of teen fashions accompanies the set containing two dolls. **g.**

Two dolls along with a wardrobe of teen fashions and movie costumes complete this set of *Judy Garland Cut-Out Dolls* #980, issued by the Whitman Publishing Company, 1941. **b.** cut; **g.** uncut

The February 1941 issue of *Screen Life* magazine featured this paper doll set along with five original outfits. **d.**

Movie Fashions paper dolls, printed by the *Chicago Sunday Tribune*. A series of single-sheet dolls and costumes illustrated by Margot. Judy Garland and Mickey Rooney paper dolls were issued on March 16, 1941. **c.**

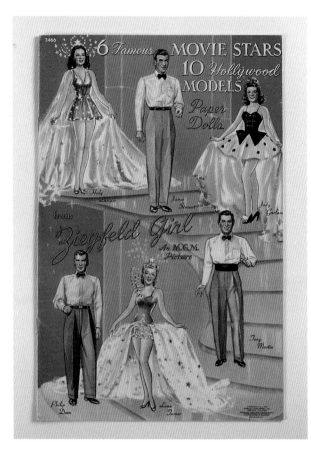

Ziegfeld Girl paper dolls featured 6 Famous MOVIE STARS, 10 Hollywood MODELS #3466. Published in 1941, by the Merrill Publishing Company, Chicago, Illinois. Set features Hedy Lamarr, James Stewart, Judy Garland, Tony Martin, Lana Turner, and Philip Dorn. **h.**

Set #996, published in 1945, by the Whitman Publishing Company. **g.**

Illustrator Tom Tierney, created this set of three JUDY GARLAND Paper Dolls in Full Color published in 1982, by Dover Publications, Inc. With remarkable accuracy and attention to detail, 30 motion picture and stage costumes complete this set. **b.**

Gay Purr-ee PUNCH-OUT FIGURES, published by Golden Press, Inc. ©1962, by U.P.A. Pictures, Inc. **b.**

Novelty Items & Books

Celebrity related merchandise reached an all time high with the Shirley Temple product licensing bonanza of the 1930s. Netting the star earnings far greater than her studio salary, her phenomenal marketing campaign established a growing trend in celebrity-related products throughout the 1930s and 40s. Still manufactured today, Judy Garland movie tie-in merchandise and novelty items, which began in the fall of 1939 with *Oz* related merchandise, continues to capture the public's imagination.

Audience members attending one of the East Coast personal appearances made by Mickey Rooney and Judy Garland, in promotion of the motion pictures *The Wizard of Oz* and *Babes in Arms*, in 1939, received a free pin-back button. Awarding special prizes as a part of the film's promotional campaign, theater owners often distributed numbered buttons to identify contest winners. Manufactured by the Philadelphia Badge Company. **c.** each

Autographed photo inscribed "To Irwin, Judy Garland." **i.**

Autographed photo inscribed "For my friends in Turkey. Best wishes always, Judy Garland. 7/1940." **i.**

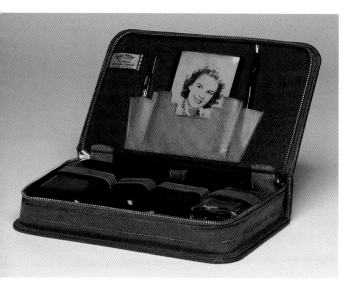

12-Pc. U.S. Seal Kit
Ideal for service men! Brown Steergrain genuine Leather kit with the Great Seal of the United States embossed on top. Zipper fastener; waterproof lining.
Contains: Large utility case, razor ·case, tooth brush box, lotion bottle, military brush, comb, shoe horn, tweezers, nail file, cuticle pusher, facial tool and mirror with photo back.
10⅜x6½x1¾ in. Brown or Black fittings. State color and 3 initials for case.
D5F 1704.......... **$2.98**

Low Priced Travel Kit
A fine gift for travelling or use at home. Genuine Leather in an elephant grain finish. Zipper fastener; waterproof lining.
Contains: Soap box, lotion bottle, tooth brush box, razor box, military brush, comb, cuticle pusher, nail file, manicure tool, tweezer and mirror with picture frame back.
Black fittings in Black or Brown case, 9¾x6x1¾ in. State color and 3 initials to be printed in gold leaf.
D5F 1703.......... **$1.98**

Military Brush Set
• Two 4⅜ x 2½-inch brushes
• 5¼ x 1¾-inch clothes brush
• 7-inch comb
A gift to please the man who is careful of his appearance.
The three brushes have genuine Leather backs with an air-plane embossed on them. Gold color metal fittings. Set with high quality White bristles. The comb is made of hard black rubber. In gift case.
D5F 1707. Complete. **$1.69**
Spiegel • 79

Judy Garland was featured on the mirror photo back of this "Genuine Leather Travel Kit" manufactured by "BAK-PROP." Offered in 1940, by the Spiegel catalog company, the kit contains: a soap box, lotion bottle, tooth brush box, razor box, military brush, comb, cuticle pusher, nail file, manicure tool, tweezers, and mirror. **e.**

Judy Garland Fashion Paint Book (#674). Published by the Whitman Publishing Company, 1940. **d.**

The Bel Air residence of Judy Garland was featured in the "Home of the Movie Stars" postcard series, published by the Longshaw Card Company, 1940. **a.**

Beginning in 1940, fashion-conscious young ladies could "DRESS LIKE A STAR in *Judy Garland's* FAVORITE DRESSES." Offered by the Montgomery Ward Christmas catalog, Denver, Colorado. **f.**

Paint Book from Ziegfeld Girl (#3465). Published by the Merrill Publishing Company, 1941. **e.**

Above : *Judy Garland Paint Book* (#601). Published by the Whitman Publishing Company, 1941. **d.**

Above Center: The *Better Little Book* series from the Whitman Publishing Company, featured *Mickey Rooney and Judy Garland*, in 1941. **b.**

Above Right: *Presenting Lily Mars* by Booth Tarkington. Motion picture edition published by Triangle Books, by arrangement with Double Day, Doran & Co., Inc., April 1943. **b.**

Three 1940s writing tablets and note pads featuring Judy Garland cover art. Publisher unknown. **b.** each

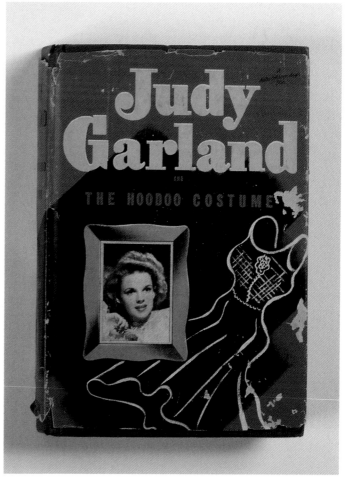

Meet Me in St. Louis by Sally Benson. "Books into Movies" series published by the World Publishing Company, in 1944. Jacket design by Leo Manso. **c.**

The Whitman Publishing Company offered readers this fictionalized adventure entitled *Judy Garland and The Hoodoo Costume*, in 1945. **b.**

"Seein' Stars Stamp" featured in Sunday newspaper comic-strip sections, circa 1944. **a.**

The Dixie Cup Company, of Chicago, Illinois, featured famous Hollywood stars on the lids of their packaging throughout the mid 1940s. This 3-ounce container lid was produced for Abbotts Ice Cream. **a.**

Series of 1940s cigarette premium cards, offered by Gallaher Ltd., London & Belfast. The reverse side of these cards often featured brief biographies and film credits along with an autograph facsimile of the star. **a.** each

Many 1940s corner drugstores featured scales where, for the price a penny, you could weigh yourself and have your fortune told, as printed on the back of a movie star portrait card. Manufactured by Printicks of Movie Stars and Engrav-o-tints Portaits of Movie Stars. **a.** each

Postcards promoting Judy Garland in *The Harvey Girls*, 1946. **a.**

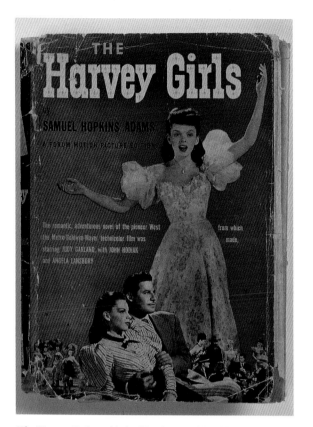

Hand-tinted color postcards featuring the glamorous Judy Garland, circa 1948. **a.**

The Harvey Girls, published by the World Publishing Company. "Books into Movies" series, 1946. **b.**

Greeting card manufactured by Stardust Greetings. © Inscription reads "Happy Birthday to one of my all time favorites. **a.**

Postcards featuring various MGM publicity photographs of Judy Garland were marketed throughout the 1940s and are still being printed and offered for sale in gift shops today. **a.**

Sara Lee, sponsors of the CBS Television series *The Judy Garland Show*, issued this promotional plastic badge to company employees, in the fall of 1963. **a.**

We're So Nice To Hug

1 **Fox Terrier on Wheels**—will "run" along at your side as you lead him on plastic leash. Squeaker voice. Lightweight, hollow body with white plush, brown and black markings. Ship. wt. 1 lb. Imported.
48 T 7129 . . . . **$2.69**

2 **"Ruff" the Puppy** with a Come-Hug-Me look on his yellow and brown plush face. Cuddly yellow body, brown ears; red felt tongue, black pompon nose; large appealing black eyes. About 16 in. tall.
48 T 6712—Ship. wt. 1 lb. **$2.99**

3 **Mewsette, the Movie Glamour Kitten**, of pure white plush with shell-pink ears and unforgettable violet felt eyes. She has long black felt eyelashes, with a pink satin bow around her neck, a "diamond" earring in one ear. About 15 in. tall.
48 T 6699—Ship. wt. 9 oz. **$3.97**

4 **"Spots"—Bold and Brave Leopard**, but yet so tame. Finest quality plush printed with markings of a Congo Leopard. Green eyes, decorated collar. About 18 in.
48 T 6713—Wt. 2 lbs. **$4.99**

"Mewsette, the Movie Glamour Kitten," as portrayed by Judy Garland in the animated feature film *Gay Purr-ee*. The 15-inch plush toy was offered for Christmas in 1963, by Montgomery Ward. **e.**

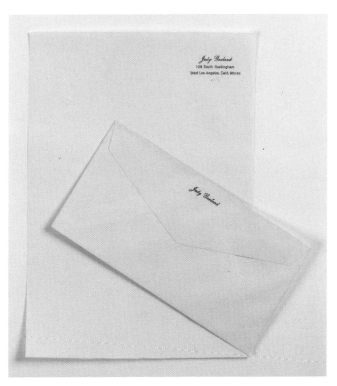

Judy Garland's personal stationary from 129 South Rockingham, West Los Angeles, California 90049. **b.**

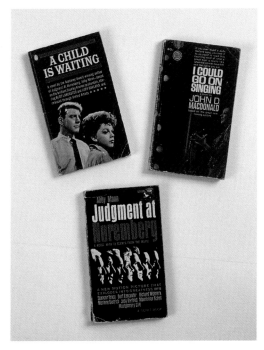

Above: Motion Picture edition paperback books. *Judgment at Nuremberg* by Abby Mann, a Signet Book © 1961. *A Child Is Waiting* by Abby Mann, Popular Library Books © 1963. *I Could Go On Singing* by John D. MacDonald, Gold Medal Books © 1963. **a** each.

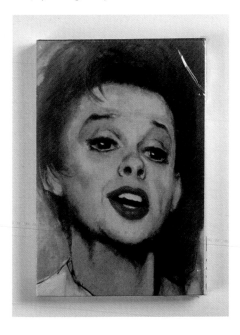

Poster puzzle entitled *Judy at the Palace*. Manufactured by International Polygonics, Inc. © 1976. From original artwork by artist Roberto Gari. 500 pieces, measuring 15 inches x 21 inches. **c.**

Judy Garland wrist-watch, circa 1976.
Maker unknown. **d.**

CARDESIGN © created this "Judy Garland" pop-up card as part of their "3 DEES" series in 1982. Illustrated by artist Kazuhiko Sano. **a.**

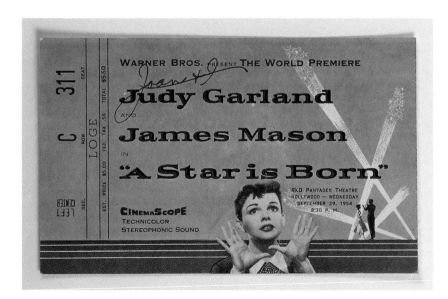

Original ticket and program, from the world premiere of *A Star Is Born*, RKO Pantages Theater, September 29, 1954. **b.** each

Above: First in the series of "Official Stamps of the Stars and Studios" featuring Charlie Chaplin, Mickey Rooney, Helen Hayes, Janet Gaynor, Edgar Bergen and Charlie McCarthy, Judy Garland, Shirley Temple, Deanna Durbin, and Jean Hersholt. **b.** set

Above Center: The United States Postal Service issued this set of four "Classic Collectibles Commemorative Stamps," on March 24, 1990. Honoring Academy Award nominated motion pictures, the stamps include: *Beau Geste, Stagecoach, The Wizard of Oz,* and *Gone With the Wind.* Designed by artist Thomas Blackshear. **b.** full sheet

Above Right: *Judy Garland Born to Sing* (#GM01). Manufactured in a limited edition by Nostalgia Collectibles, 1984. Measuring 7 inches tall, the porcelain figurine features a battery operated cassette player with recordings of Judy Garland performing: "The Trolley Song," "Somewhere Over the Rainbow," "You Made Me Love You," and "Born in a Trunk." Other musical figurines in "The Talkies" collection include: Shirley Temple, Al Jolson, and Gene Kelly. **c.**

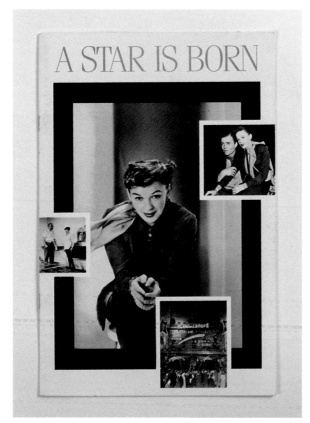

Premiere program for the restoration and reconstruction of *A Star Is Born.* Opening: New York, Thursday, July 7, 1983. Presented by the Academy of Motion Picture Arts and Sciences in cooperation with Warner Bros. **b.**

22-page program for the 1983 re-issue of *A Star Is Born,* Tokyo, Japan. **b.**

Porcelain collector's plate from the "Images of Hollywood" collection. Limited edition *Easter Parade* featuring Judy Garland and Fred Astaire. Issued in 1986. **c.**

"A Commemorative to *Judy Garland*" porcelain collector's plate. Limited edition by artist Susie Morton, manufactured by R. J. Ernest Enterprises, Inc. **c.**

Judy, by artist Jan Hilland. Second in the series of eight porcelain "Celebrity Clown Plates," manufactured by American Heritage Art Products, Ltd. **c.**

Manufacturers of replica jewelry worn by famous stars from the "golden age of Hollywood" Parkway's Hollywood Collection © offered two Judy Garland items in 1993. Left: a faux ruby and diamond ring as worn by Judy in *Babes in Arms*. Right: a faux diamond and sapphire bow pin from *Ziegfeld Girl*. **d.** each

Pre-Paid Calling Cards from Teleworld © 1994. Set of seven limited edition cards featuring photographs from the collection of Sid Luft. **c.**

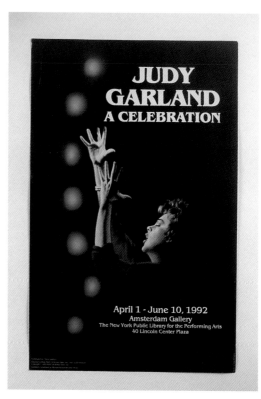

Poster art for New York's Lincoln Center exhibit "Judy Garland - A Celebration," featuring several of her original MGM costumes and related memorabilia. April 1 - June 10, 1992. **b.**

Concert Posters & Programs

Judy Garland began her concert career on April 9, 1951, with a four-week engagement at the London Palladium. A record-breaking nineteen-week run at the Palace theater in New York followed in October, which would lead to over one hundred concerts during the next eighteen years of her life.

Performing one-night stands and multi-week engagements throughout the world, Judy left "standing-room only" audiences completely spellbound. Garland "Live" was clearly more than a concert; it was an event. Awed by her formidable vocal power, dynamic personality, and showmanship, her audiences begged and cheered for more. Being the consummate entertainer, Judy would exuberantly shout back night after night, "I'll sing em' all, and we'll stay all night!"

"Palace Two-A-Day," starring Judy Garland and a All Star Variety Show. Opening: New York, October 16, 1951. Theatre program (as shown), for the week beginning Monday, February 11, 1952. Act I: The Shyrettos (Three Wonders on Wheels), Nicholas Brothers, Senor Wences, Joe Smith & Charlie Dale, and Giselle and Francois Szony. Act II: Judy Garland, with (her dancers) Judy's Eight Boy Friends. Composer Hugh Martin at the piano. **b.**

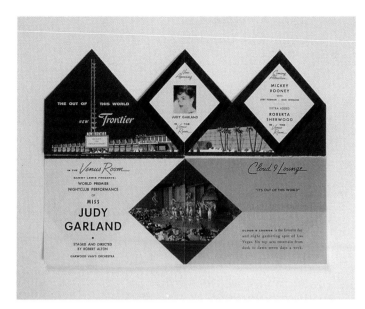

"The World Premiere Nightclub Performance of Miss Judy Garland," The New Frontier Hotel and Casino, Las Vegas, Nevada. Opening: July 16, 1956. Featuring: The Amin Brothers, The Risley Acrobatic Team, with Judy's Boy Friends. **b.**

"Judy Garland, RKO Palace Theatre" program. Opening: New York, Wednesday, September 26, 1956. Act I: Amin Brothers (Acrobatics Extraordinary), Bob Williams, Pompoff, Thedy and Family, Nora Kovach and Istvan Rabovsky, and Alan King. Act II: Judy Garland, with Judy's 12 Boy Friends. Also featuring Bert May and the Wazzan Troupe. **b.**

"The Judy Garland Show," Dominion Theatre programme, London, England. Opening: October 16, 1957. Featuring comedian Alan King. **b.**

"Miss Show Business" Judy Garland with Alan King and the Nelson Riddle Orchestra. Orchestra Hall program, Chicago, Illinois. Opening: September 4, 1958. **b.**

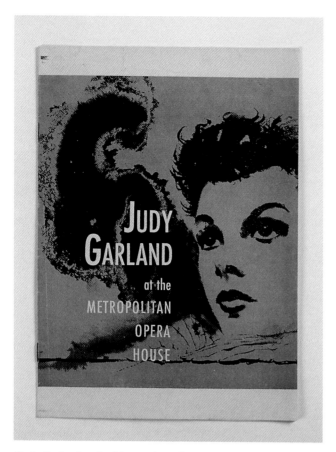

"Judy Garland at the Metropolitan Opera House" program. Opening: New York, May 11, 1959. Produced by Sid Luft. Musical direction by Gordon Jenkins. Featuring: John Bubbles and Alan King. **b.**

Festival Hall program. Opening: Melbourne, Australia, May 20, 1964. **b.**

Flyer promoting "Judy, World's Greatest Entertainer, In Person." Mosque Theatre, Newark, New Jersey. Opening: October 7, (possibly 1967). **a.**

Playbill, "Judy Garland at home at the Palace." Opening: July 31, 1967. A Group V Production, presented by Sid Luft. Cover portrait painted by Roberto Gari. The original artwork is now on display in the theater collection at the Museum of the City of New York. Act I: Francis Brunn, John Bubbles, and Jackie Vernon. Act II: Judy Garland and, introducing her protégés, Lorna and Joey Luft. **b.**

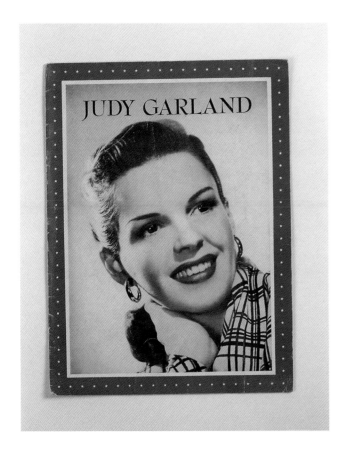

Series of four 1960s concert programs. Theatres and engagement dates
unlisted. **a.** each

Concert poster for Judy Garland's December 17, 1965, appearance at the Astrodome, Houston, Texas. Opening act: The Supremes. **f.**

Poster art for the Sunday, February 25, 1968, concert at the Philharmonic Hall, Lincoln Center, New York. **e.**

Costumes

In late 1969, Metro-Goldwyn-Mayer announced that they would begin selling property to help finance the MGM Grand Hotel and Casino, in Las Vegas, Nevada. Land parcels known as back lots 2, 3, 4, and 5 were sold to developers for condominiums, while auctioneer David Weisz handled the liquidation of all of the contents. Purchased for a price of $1.5 million, the inventory represented Louis B. Mayer's lifetime collection of antique treasures and movie memories, which included an unprecedented seven sound stages filled to capacity with props, furniture, and an estimated 350,000 costumes.

The Star Wardrobe auction, held on May 17, 1970, showcased a catalog of costumes created by the film industry's most elite fashion designers from Hollywood's "golden age." As expected, lot #W-1048 proved to be the highlight of the sale. Judy Garland's magical ruby slippers from *The Wizard of Oz* sold for a winning bid of $15,000.

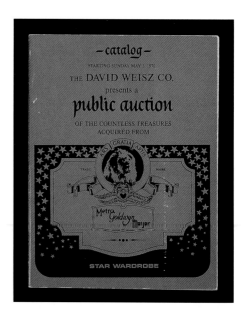

Today, nearly thirty years later, surviving costumes from the original 1970 MGM auction continue to make their way into auction houses across the country and onto the Internet as well.

The Wizard of Oz, 1939
Designer: Adrian

As "Dorothy," Judy Garland began her journey to the land of *Oz* wearing this costume consisting of a blue cotton jumper, trimmed with a polka-dot fabric detailing on the shoulder straps, chest and waist bands, and along the bottom hem. Bodice is lined in an off-white cotton with a sewn-in garment label inscribed "Judy Garland 3955." The original white organdy blouse is stamped on the inside collar "169L." The entire costume along the original makeup and hair designs was discarded after only two weeks of filming. New wardrobe tests were immediately ordered under the guidance of director George Cukor; these lead to the final results that are seen on screen. Dozens of original production stills remain from director Richard Thorpe's unused footage, shot in the witch's castle and in the cornfield along the Yellow Brick Road, leaving this extremely rare costume well documented. **k.**

The Wizard of Oz, 1939
Designer: Adrian

No less than six different dresses were designed and executed by Gilbert Adrian before *Oz* producer Mervyn LeRoy gave his final approval for Judy Garland's costume. This red polka-dot cotton jumper, labeled "169L," illustrates the progression in design, length, and color. The choice of the color red for the jumper (more than likely) was eliminated as soon as the developing screenplay changed book author L. Frank Baum's original pair of magical shoes worn by Dorothy from silver slippers to ruby slippers. If the shoes were to be red, then clearly another choice would be needed for the color of her dress. The white organdy blouse, stamped "169L," is simplified slightly from the previous one shown, although it is made from the exact pattern, size, and materials. Blouse is detailed with white rick-rack trim on the collar and sleeves. **j.**

The Wizard of Oz, 1939.
Designer: Adrian

As photographed for the 1970 MGM auction, Judy Garland's Dorothy costume from the classic MGM motion picture *The Wizard of Oz*. The blue and white gingham jumper is made of 100 % cotton, over-dyed with a pale pink tinge. Bodice is lined in off-white cotton with a sewn-in garment label inscribed "Judy Garland 4228." Jumper is shown over the original blouse used during the first two weeks of production under the direction of Richard Thorpe. For use over the many months of filming, this costume was made in duplicates, possibly as many as eight. When last offered for public sale at Sotheby's, in December 1992, costume brought $48,400. Also pictured are the original magical ruby slippers of *Oz* and the menacing hourglass of the Wicked Witch of the West. The hourglass, offered at auction in 1992, brought $66,000.

The Wizard of Oz, 1939.
Designer: Adrian

Another original, early blouse design for Dorothy. Made of organdy, trimmed with a floral lace embroidery. Stamped "169L." **i.**

The ruby slippers are made from French-heeled pumps, covered in red silk faille, overlaid with hand-sequined georgette. Inside right shoe features an embossed label reading "Innes Shoe Co. Los Angeles, Pasadena, Hollywood," along with the stamped manufacturer's numbers and size 5BC. Again made in multiples, Christie's East offered a pair for public auction in 1988, selling for $165,000.

Ziegfeld Girl, 1941.
Designer: Adrian

Created for the film's finale, an elaborate production number directed and choreographed by Busby Berkeley entitled "We Must Have Music," this majorette-style jacket was originally detailed with gold epaulets and a leather belt strapped across the chest and around the waist, trimmed with gold braiding. Tagged with a Metro-Goldwyn-Mayer costume label inscribed "Judy Garland 1165-9313." This costume along with portions of the original musical number can be seen in the 1942 MGM film short *We Must Have Music*. **i.**

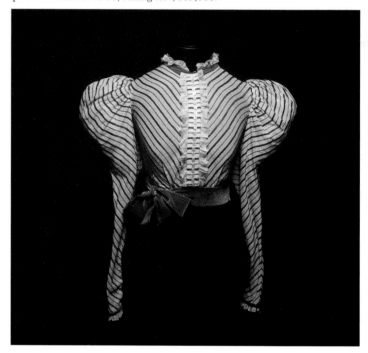

The Harvey Girls, 1946.
Designer: Helen Rose, supervised by Irene

Blouse is made of a light cotton with embroidered red stripes, trimmed with green velvet and lace. Sewn-in garment tag reads "Judy Garland 1348." As the character Susan Bradley, this costume is worn by Judy when she receives her "first kiss" from love interest Ned Trent, played by actor John Hodiak. **i.**

The Pirate, 1948.
Designer: Irene, executed by Karinska

A stunning example of the craftsmanship of the MGM costume department. Made from the finest velvet and imported French silk, this elaborate gown, tagged with a Metro-Goldwyn-Mayer label, is inscribed "Judy Garland 1400 Change #7." Costume is worn in the motion picture for the musical number "Love of My Life," which is sung to the about-to-be executed Serafin, alias Mack the Black, played by Gene Kelly. The original petticoat, consisting of seven layers of orange and white lace, accompanies the gown. **k.**

In the Good Old Summertime, 1949.
Designer: Irene

This pleated skirt, with a sewn-in garment label inscribed "1440-5841 J. Garland," is worn throughout the film in several key scenes, including the musical numbers "Put Your Arms Around Me Honey" and "Merry Christmas." **i.**

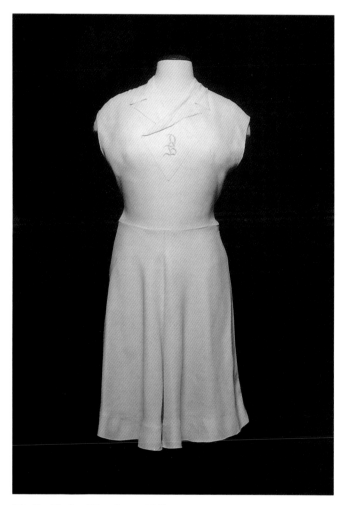

The Barkley's of Broadway, 1949.
Designer: Irene

Exhausted and overworked, Judy Garland was fired from this production and immediately replaced by Ginger Rogers. This sleeveless, cream-colored chiffon dancing dress survives, monogrammed with the initials "D B" (Dinah Barkley). Sewn-in garment label reads "1433-5337 J. Garland." **h.**

Motion Picture Chronology

Shorts

The Big Review
Mayfair Pictures
Released: 1929
Running time: One reel, 10 minutes
Cast: The Meglin Kiddies, featuring the Gumm Sisters performing "The Good Old Sunny South."

A Holiday in Storyland
First National-Vitaphone Pictures
Released: 1930
Running time: One reel, 10 minutes
Cast: The Hollywood Starlets, featuring the Gumm Sisters billed as the Three Kute Kiddies, performing "Where the Butterflies Kiss the Buttercups" and, as a solo, Baby Gumm singing "Blue Butterfly."

The Wedding of Jack and Jill
First National-Vitaphone Pictures
Released: 1930
Running time: One reel, 10 minutes
Cast: The Hollywood Starlets, featuring Baby Gumm performing "Hang on to a Rainbow."

Bubbles
First National-Vitaphone Pictures
Released: 1930
Running time: One reel, 10 minutes
Cast: The Hollywood Starlets, featuring Baby Gumm performing "Lady Luck."

La Fiesta de Santa Barbara
Metro-Goldwyn-Mayer
Released: 1935
Running time: One reel, 10 minutes
Cast: Warner Baxter, Ralph Forbes, featuring Buster Keaton, Ida Lupino, Binnie Barnes, Les Carillo, Shirley Ross, Harpo Marx, and the Garland Sisters performing "La Cucaracha."
This film short marked the final performance of the Gumm Sisters.

Every Sunday
Metro-Goldwyn-Mayer
Released: 1936
Running time: Two reels, 20 minutes
Directed by Felix E. Feist
Screenplay by Mauri Grashin
Cast: Judy Garland, Deanna Durbin, featuring Judy Garland performing "America."

Christmas
Metro-Goldwyn-Mayer
Released: 1937
Running time: One reel, 10 minutes
Cast: Featuring Judy Garland performing "Silent Night."

We Must Have Music
Metro-Goldwyn-Mayer
Released: 1942
Running time: One reel, 10 minutes
Cast: Featuring Judy Garland performing the title song "We Must Have Music."
Directed by Busby Berkeley, this number was cut from the finale of *Ziegfeld Girl*.

Features

Pigskin Parade
20th Century-Fox
Released: 1936
Running time: 95 minutes
Produced by Darryl F. Zanuck
Directed by David Butler
Screenplay by Harry Tugend, Jack Yellen, William Conselman
Music and Lyrics by Lew Pollack, Sidney Mitchell, The Yacht Club Boys
Costumes by Gwen Wakeling

Cast
Amos Dodd	Stuart Erwin
Bessie Winters	Patsy Kelly
Slug Winters	Jack Haley
The Yacht Club Boys	Themselves
Chip Carson	Johnny Downs
Laura Watson	Betty Grable
Sally Saxon	Arline Judge
Ginger Jones	Dixie Dunbar
Sairy Dodd	Judy Garland
Tommy Baker	Anthony Martin
Biff Bentley	Fred Kohler, Jr.
Mortimer Higgins	Grady Sutton
Herbert Van Dyke	Elisha Cook, Jr.
Sparks	Eddie Nugent
Dr. Burke	Julius Tannen

Broadway Melody of 1938
Metro-Goldwyn-Mayer
Released: 1937
Running time: 113 minutes
Produced by Jack Cummings
Directed by Roy Del Ruth
Screenplay by Jack McGowan, from an original story by Jack McGowan and Sid Silvers
Music and Lyrics by Nacio Herb Brown and Arthur Freed
Costumes by Adrian
Cast
Steve Raleigh	Robert Taylor
Sally Lee	Eleanor Powell
Sonny Ledford	George Murphy
Caroline Whipple	Binnie Barnes
Peter Trot	Buddy Ebsen
Alice Clayton	Sophie Tucker
Betty Clayton	Judy Garland
Nicki Simonini	Charles Igor Gorin
Herman Whipple	Raymond Walburn
Duff	Robert Benchley
with Willie Howard, Charles Grapewin, Robert Wildhack, Billy Gilbert, Barnett Parker, Helen Troy

Thoroughbreds Don't Cry
Metro-Goldwyn-Mayer
Released: 1938
Running time: 80 minutes
Produced by Harry Rapf
Directed by Alfred E. Green
Screenplay by Lawrence Hazard, from an original story by Eleanor Griffen and J. Walter Ruben
Music and Lyrics by Nacio Herb Brown and Arthur Freed
Costumes by Dolly Tree
Cast
Cricket West	Judy Garland
Timmy Donahue	Mickey Rooney
Mother Ralph	Sophie Tucker
Sir Peter Calverton	C. Aubrey Smith
Roger Calverton	Robert Sinclair
Hilda	Helen Troy
"Click" Donahue	Charles D. Brown
Dink Reid	Frankie Darro
"Doc" Godfrey	Henry Kolker
Wilkins	Forrester Harvey

Everybody Sing
Metro-Goldwyn-Mayer
Released: 1938
Running time: 80 minutes
Produced by Harry Rapf
Directed by Edwin L. Marin
Screenplay by Florence Ryerson, Edgar Allen Woolf, James Gruen
Music and Lyrics by Walter Jurmann and Gus Kahn, Bert Kalmer and Harry Ruby
Costumes by Dolly Tree

Cast

Ricky Saboni	Allan Jones
Judy Bellaire	Judy Garland
Olga Chekalof	Fanny Brice
Hillary Bellair	Reginald Owen
Diana Bellaire	Billie Burke
Jerrold Hope	Reginald Gardiner
Sylvia Bellaire	Lynne Carver
Hillary's secretary	Helen Troy
John Fleming	Monty Woolley
Boris	Adia Kuznetzoff
Signor Vittorino	Henry Armetta
Madame Le Brouchette	Michelette Burani
Miss Colvin	Mary Forbes

Listen, Darling

Metro-Goldwyn-Mayer
Released: 1938
Running time: 70 minutes
Produced by Jack Cummings
Directed by Edwin L. Marin
Screenplay by Elaine Ryan and Anne Morrison Chapin, from a story by Katherine Brush
Music and Lyrics by Al Hoffman, Al Lewis and Murray Mencher, Joseph McCarthy, Milton Ager and James F. Henley
Costumes by Dolly Tree
Cast

"Pinkie" Wingate	Judy Garland
"Buzz" Mitchell	Freddie Bartholomew
Dottie Wingate	Mary Astor
Richard Thurlow	Walter Pidgeon
J.J. Slattery	Alan Hale
Billie Wingate	Scotty Beckett
Abercrombie	Barnett Parker
Mr. Drubbs	Gene Lockhart
Uncle Joe	Charley Grapewin

Love Finds Andy Hardy

Metro-Goldwyn-Mayer
Released: 1938
Running time: 90 minutes
Produced by Lou Ostrow
Directed by George B. Seitz
Screenplay by William Ludwig, from stories by Vivien R. Bretherton, and characters created by Aurania Rouverol
Music and Lyrics by Mack Gordon and Harry Revel, Roger Edens
Costumes by Jeanne
Cast

Judge James Hardy	Lewis Stone
Andy Hardy	Mickey Rooney
Marian Hardy	Cecilia Parker
Mrs. Hardy	Fay Holden
Betsy	Judy Garland
Cynthia	Lana Turner
Polly Benedict	Ann Rutherford
Mrs. Tompkins	Mary Howard
Jimmy McMahon	Gene Reynolds
Dennis Hunt	Don Castle
Aunt Milly	Betty Ross Clarke
Augusta	Marie Blake
"Beezy"	George Breakstone
Peter Dugan	Raymond Hatton
Bill Collector	Frank Darien

The Wizard of Oz

Metro-Goldwyn-Mayer
Released: 1939
Running time: 100 minutes
Produced by Mervyn LeRoy
Directed by Victor Fleming
Screenplay by Noel Langley, Florence Ryerson, and Edgar Allan Woolf, from the book by L. Frank Baum
Music and Lyrics by Harold Arlen and E.Y. Harburg
Costumes by Adrian
Cast

Dorothy	Judy Garland
Professor Marvel	Frank Morgan
"Hunk"	Ray Bolger
"Zeke"	Bert Lahr
"Hickory"	Jack Haley
Glinda	Billie Burke
Miss Gulch	Margaret Hamilton
Uncle Henry	Charlie Grapewin
Nikko	Pat Walshe
Auntie Em	Clara Blandick
Toto	Toto

with The Singer Midgets as the Munchkins

Babes in Arms

Metro-Goldwyn-Mayer
Released: 1939
Running time: 91 minutes
Produced by Arthur Freed
Directed by Busby Berkeley
Screenplay by Jack McGowan and Kay Van Riper, from a play by Richard Rodgers and Lorenz Hart
Music and Lyrics by Richard Rodgers and Lorenz Hart, Nacio Herb Brown and Arthur Freed, Harold Arlen and E.Y. Harburg
Costumes by Dolly Tree
Cast

Mickey Moran	Mickey Rooney
Patsy Barton	Judy Garland
Joe Moran	Charles Winninger
Judge Black	Guy Kibbee
Rosalie Essex	June Preisser
Florrie Moran	Grace Hayes
Molly Moran	Betty Jaynes
Don Brice	Douglas McPhail
Jeff Steele	Rand Brooks
Dody Martini	Leni Lynn
Bobs	John Sheffield
Maddox	Henry Hull
William	Barnet Parker
Mrs. Barton	Ann Shoemaker
Martha Steele	Margaret Hamilton
Mr. Essex	Joseph Crehan
Brice	George McKay
Shaw	Henry Roquemore
Mrs. Brice	Lelah Tyler

For use in publications such as Metro-Goldwyn-Mayer's in-house magazine the *Lion's Roar*, artist Jacques Kapralik created three-dimensional publicity art for many of Judy Garland's motion pictures. Illustrated here Mickey Rooney and Judy Garland in *Andy Hardy Meets Debutante.* **b.**

Andy Hardy Meets Debutante
Metro-Goldwyn-Mayer
Released: 1940
Running time: 87 minutes
Produced by Carey Wilson
Directed by George B. Seitz
Screenplay by Annalee Whitmore and Thomas Seller, from characters created by Aurania Rouverol
Musical Score by David Snell
Musical Arrangements by Roger Edens and Georgie Stoll
Costumes by Dolly Tree
Cast
Judge James Hardy .... Lewis Stone
Andy Hardy .... Mickey Rooney
Marian Hardy .... Cecilia Parker
Mrs. Hardy .... Fay Holden
Betsy Booth .... Judy Garland
Polly Benedict .... Ann Rutherford
Dyanne Fowler .... Diana Lewis
"Beezy" .... George Breakstone
Aunt Milly .... Sara Haden
with Harry Tyler, Cy Kendall, Addison Richards, George Lessey, Gladys Blake, Clyde Willson

Strike Up the Band
Metro-Goldwyn-Mayer
Released: 1940
Running time: 120 minutes
Produced by Arthur Freed
Directed by Busby Berkeley
Screenplay by John Monks, Jr. and Fred Finklehoffe
Music and Lyrics by Roger Edens, George and Ira Gershwin, Arthur Freed
Costumes by Dolly Tree
Cast
Jimmy Connors .... Mickey Rooney
Mary Holden .... Judy Garland
Paul Whiteman .... Himself
Barbara Frances Morgan .... June Preisser
Philip Turner .... William Tracy
Willie Brewster .... Larry Nunn
Annie .... Margaret Early
Mrs. Connors .... Ann Shoemaker
Mr. Judd .... Francis Pierlot
Mrs. Hoden .... Virginia Brissac
with George Lessey, Enid Bennett, Howard Hickman, Sarah Edwards, Milton Kibbee, Helen Jerome Eddy

Kapralik art for *Strike Up the Band.* **b.**

Little Nellie Kelly
Metro-Goldwyn-Mayer
Released: 1940
Running time: 96 minutes
Produced by Arthur Freed
Directed by Norman Taurog
Screenplay by Jack McGowan, based on a musical comedy by George M. Cohan
Music and Lyrics by George M. Cohan, Nacio Herb Brown, Arthur Freed, Roger Edens
Costumes by Dolly Tree, Gile Steele
Cast
Nellie Kelly/Little Nellie Kelly .... Judy Garland
Jerry Kelly .... George Murphy
Michael Noonan .... Charles Winninger
Dennis Fogarty .... Douglas McPhail
Timothy Fogarty .... Arthur Shields
Mary Fogarty .... Rita Page
Moriarity .... Forrester Harvey
Sergeant McGowan .... James Burke
Keevan .... George Watts
with Robert Homans, Thomas P. Dillon, Henry Blair

Kapralik art for *Little Nellie Kelly.* **b.**

Ziegfeld Girl
Metro-Goldwyn-Mayer
Released: 1941
Running time: 135 minutes
Produced by Pandro S. Berman
Directed by Robert Z. Leonard
Screenplay by Marguerite Roberts and Sonya Levien, from a story by William Anthony McGuire
Music and Lyrics by Nacio Herb Brown, Gus Kahn, Roger Edens, Antonio and Rosanio, Harry Carroll, Joseph McCarthy, Edward Gallagher, Al Shean
Costumes by Adrian
Cast
Gilbert Young .... James Stewart
Susan Gallagher .... Judy Garland
Sandra Kolter .... Hedy Lamarr
Sheila Regan .... Lana Turner
Frank Merton .... Tony Martin
Jerry Regan .... Jackie Cooper
Geoffrey Collis .... Ian Hunter
"Pop" Gallagher .... Charles Winninger
Noble Sage .... Edward Everett Horton
Franz Kolter .... Philip Dorn
with Paul Kelly, Eve Arden, Dan Dailey, Jr., Al Shean, Fay Holden, Felix

Bressart, Rose Hobart, Bernard Nedell, Ed McNamara, Mae Bush, Renie Riano, Josephine Whittell, Sergio Orta

Life Begins for Andy Hardy
Metro-Goldwyn-Mayer
Released: 1941
Running time: 100 minutes
Produced by Carey Wilson, J.J. Cohn
Directed by George B. Seitz
Screenplay by Agnes Christine Johnston, based on characters created by Aurania Rouverol
Musical Direction by Georgie Stoll
Costumes by Kalloch
Cast
Judge James Hardy .... Lewis Stone
Andy Hardy .... Mickey Rooney
Betsy Booth .... Judy Garland
Mrs. Hardy .... Fay Holden
Polly Benedict .... Ann Rutherford
Aunt Milly .... Sara Haden
Jennitt Hicks .... Patricia Dane
Jimmy Frobisher .... Ray McDonald
"Beezy" .... George Breakstone
Dr. Waggoner .... Pierre Watkin

Kapralik art for *Life Begins for Andy Hardy.* **b.**

Babes on Broadway
Metro-Goldwyn-Mayer
Released: 1941
Running time: 118 minutes
Produced by Arthur Freed
Directed by Busby Berkeley
Screenplay by Fred Finklehoffe and Elaine Ryan
Music and Lyrics by E.Y. Harburg, Burton Lane, Ralph Freed, Roger Edens, Harold Rome
Costumes by Kalloch
Cast
Tommy Williams .... Mickey Rooney
Penny Morris .... Judy Garland
Miss Jones .... Fay Bainter
Barbara Jo .... Virginia Weidler
Ray Lambert .... Ray McDonald
Morton Hammond .... Richard Quine
Mr. Stone .... Donald Meek
Alexander Woollcott .... Himself
Thorton Reed .... James Gleason

Mrs. Williams .... Emma Dunn
Mr. Morris .... Frederick Burton
Inspector Moriarity .... Cliff Clark
Secretary .... Donna Reed
with Luis Alberni, Ava Gardner, William Pool, Jr., Roger Moore, Six Hits and a Miss

Kapralik art for *Babes on Broadway.* **b.**

For Me and My Gal
Metro-Goldwyn-Mayer
Released: 1942
Running time: 104 minutes
Produced by Arthur Freed
Directed by Busby Berkeley
Screenplay by Richard Sherman, Fred Finklehoffe, Sid Silvers, based on a story by Howard Emmett Rogers
Music and Lyrics by George W. Meyer, Edgar Leslie, E. Ray Goetz
Costumes by Kalloch
Cast
Jo Hayden .... Judy Garland
Jimmy Metcalf .... George Murphy
Harry Palmer .... Gene Kelly
Eve Minard .... Marta Eggerth
Sid Simms .... Ben Blue
Danny Hayden .... Richard Quine
Bert Waring .... Horace McNally
Lily .... Lucille Norman
Eddie Melton .... Keenan Wynn

Presenting Lily Mars
Metro-Goldwyn-Mayer
Released: 1943
Running time: 105 minutes
Produced by Joe Pasternak
Directed by Norman Taurog
Screenplay by Richard Connell and Gladys Lehman, based on a novel by Booth Tarkington
Music and Lyrics by Walter Jurmann, Paul Francis Webster, E.Y. Harburg, Burton Lane, Roger Edens
Costumes by Howard Shoup
Cast
Lily Mars .... Judy Garland
John Thornway .... Van Heflin
Mrs. Thornway .... Fay Bainter
Owen Vail .... Richard Carlson

Kapralik art for *For Me and My Gal*. **b.**

Kapralik art for *Presenting Lily Mars*. **b.**

Kapralik art for *Girl Crazy*. **b.**

Mrs. Mars .... Spring Byington
Isobel Rekay .... Marta Eggerth
Frankie .... Connie Gilchrist
Leo .... Leonid Kinskey
Poppy .... Patricia Barker
Violet .... Janet Chapman
Rosie .... Annabelle Logan
Davey .... Douglas Croft
Charlie Potter .... Ray McDonald
with Tommy Dorsey and his orchestra, Bob Crosby and his orchestra

Girl Crazy
Metro-Goldwyn-Mayer
Released: 1943
Running time: 100 minutes
Produced by Arthur Freed
Directed by Norman Taurog
Screenplay by Fred Finklehoffe, based on a play by Guy Bolton and Jack McGowan
Music and Lyrics by George and Ira Gershwin
Costumes by Irene
Cast
Danny Churchill, Jr. .... Mickey Rooney
Ginger Gray .... Judy Garland
Bud Livermore .... Gil Stratton
Henry Lathrop .... Robert E. Strickland
"Rags" .... Rags Ragland
Polly Williams .... Nancy Walker
Dean Phineas Armour .... Guy Kibbee
Marjorie Tait .... Frances Rafferty
Governor Tait .... Howard Freeman
Mr. Churchill, Sr. .... Henry O'Neill
with Tommy Dorsey and his orchestra, June Allyson

Thousands Cheer
Metro-Goldwyn-Mayer
Released: 1943
Running time: 126 minutes
Produced by Joe Pasternak
Directed by George Sidney
Screenplay by Paul Jarrico and Richard Collins
Music and Lyrics by Ferde Grofe, Harold Adamson, Lew Brown, Ralph Freed, Burton Lane, Walter Jurmann, Paul Francis Webster, Earle Brent, E.Y. Harburg, Dimitri Shostakovich, Harold Rome
Costumes by Irene
Cast
Kathryn Jones .... Kathryn Grayson
Eddie Marsh .... Gene Kelly
Hyllary Jones .... Mary Astor
Colonel William Jones .... John Boles
Chuck Polansky .... Ben Blue
Marie Corbino .... Frances Rafferty
Helen .... Mary Elliott
Sgt. Kozlack .... Frank Jenks
Alan .... Frank Sully
Captain Fred Avery .... Dick Simmons
Pvt. Monks .... Ben Lessy
Jose Iturbi .... Himself
Guest Appearances By: Judy Garland, Mickey Rooney, Red Skelton, Eleanor Powell, Lucille Ball, Ann Sothern, Virginia O'Brien, Frank Morgan, Lena Horne, Marsha Hunt, Marilyn Maxwell, Donna Reed, Margaret O'Brien, June Allyson, Gloria DeHaven, John Conte, Sara Haden, Don Loper, Maxine Barrat, Kay Kyser and his orchestra, Bob Crosby and his orchestra, Benny Carter and his band
Featuring Judy Garland singing "The Joint Is Really Jumpin' Down at Carnegie Hall"

Meet Me in St. Louis
Metro-Goldwyn-Mayer
Released: 1944
Running time: 114 minutes
Produced by Arthur Freed
Directed by Vincente Minnelli
Screenplay by Irving Brecher and Fred Finklehoffe, based on the book by Sally Benson
Music and Lyrics by Hugh Martin and Ralph Blane
Costumes by Sharaff
Cast
Esther Smith .... Judy Garland
"Tootie" Smith .... Margaret O'Brien

Kapralik art for *The Clock*. **b.**

Mrs. Anna Smith	Mary Astor
Rose Smith	Lucille Bremer
Mr. Alonzo Smith	Leon Ames
John Truett	Tom Drake
Katie (Maid)	Marjorie Main
Granpa	Harry Davenport
Lucille Ballard	June Lockhart
Lon Smith, Jr.	Henry Daniels, Jr.
Agnes Smith	Joan Carroll
Colonel Darly	Hugh Marlowe
Warren Sheffield	Robert Sully
Mr. Neely	Chill Wills

The Clock
Metro-Goldwyn-Mayer
Released: 1945
Running time: 90 minutes
Produced by Arthur Freed
Directed by Vincente Minnelli
Screenplay by Robert Nathan and Joseph Schrank, based on a story by Paul and Pauline Gallico
Musical Score by George Bassman
Costumes by Irene and Marion Herwood Keyes
Cast

Alice Mayberry	Judy Garland
Corporal Joe Allen	Robert Walker
Al Henry	James Gleason
Drunk	Keenan Wynn
Bill	Marshall Thompson
Mrs. Al Henry	Lucille Gleason
Helen	Ruth Brady
Woman in restaurant	Moyna Macgill

The Harvey Girls
Metro-Goldwyn-Mayer
Released: 1946
Running time: 101 minutes
Produced by Arthur Freed
Directed by George Sidney
Screenplay by Edmund Beloin, Nathaniel Curtis, Harry Crane, James O'Hanlon, Samson Raphaelson, based on a book by Samuel Hopkins Adams, story by Eleanore Griffin and William Rankin
Music and Lyrics by Harry Warren and Johnny Mercer
Costumes by Helen Rose, Valles, supervised by Irene
Cast

Susan Bradley	Judy Garland
Ned Trent	John Hodiak
Chris Maule	Ray Bolger
Em	Angela Lansbury
Judge Sam Purvis	Preston Foster
Alma	Virginia O'Brien
Terry O'Halloran	Kenny Baker
Sonora Cassidy	Marjorie Main
H.H. Hartsey	Chill Wills
Miss Bliss	Selena Royle
Deborah	Cyd Charisse
Ethel	Ruth Brady

with Jack Lambert, Edward Earle, Morris Ankrum, William Phillips, Ben Carter, Norman Leavitt, Horace McNally

Ziegfeld Follies
Metro-Goldwyn-Mayer
Released: 1946
Running time: 109 minutes
Produced by Arthur Freed
Directed by Vincente Minnelli, George Sidney, Robert Lewis, Lemuel Ayers, Roy Del Ruth
Musical Direction by Lennie Hayton
Costumes by Irene and Helen Rose
Cast: Fred Astaire, Lucille Ball, Lucille Bremer, Fanny Brice, Cyd Charisse, Judy Garland, Kathryn Grayson, Lena Horne, Gene Kelly, Red Skelton, Esther Williams
with James Melton, Victor Moore, Marion Bell, Edward Arnold, Ray Teal, Naomi Childers, Hume Cronyn, William Frawley, Robert Lewis, Harriet Lee, Rex Evans, the Bunin Puppets, featuring Judy Garland performing "A Great Lady Has an Interview"

Till the Clouds Roll By
Metro-Goldwyn-Mayer
Released: 1946
Running time: 120 minutes
Produced by Arthur Freed
Directed by Richard Whorf, (Judy Garland sequences directed by Vincente Minnelli)
Music by Jerome Kern
Costumes by Helen Rose, Valles, supervised by Irene
Cast
Jerome Kern .... Robert Walker
Marilyn Miller .... Judy Garland
Sally .... Lucille Bremer
James I. Hessler .... Van Heflin
Oscar Hammerstein .... Paul Langton
Mrs. Jerome Kern .... Dorothy Patrick
Mrs. Muller .... Mary Nash
Bandleader .... Van Johnson
Julie Sanderson .... Dinah Shore
Charles Frohman .... Harry Hayden
Victor Herbert .... Paul Macey
Sally, as a girl .... Joan Wells
with June Allyson, Cyd Charisse, Gower Champion, Kathryn Grayson, Lena Horne, Angela Lansbury, Tony Martin, Ray McDonald, Virginia O'Brien, Caleb Peterson, William Phillips, Frank Sinatra, the Wilde Twins

The Pirate
Metro-Goldwyn-Mayer
Released: 1948
Running time: 102 minutes
Produced by Arthur Freed
Directed by Vincente Minnelli
Screenplay by Albert Hackett and Frances Goodrich, based on a play by S. N. Behrman
Music and Lyrics by Cole Porter
Costumes by Tom Keogh, executed by Karinska, supervised by Irene
Cast
Manuela .... Judy Garland
Serafin .... Gene Kelly
Don Pedro Vargas .... Walter Slezak
Aunt Inez .... Gladys Cooper
The Advocate .... Reginald Owen
The Viceroy .... George Zucco
Specialty Danc .... The Nicholas Brothers
Uncle Capucho .... Lester Allen
Isabella .... Lola Deem
Mercedes .... Ellen Ross
Lizarda .... Mary Jo Ellis
Casilda .... Jean Dean
with Marion Murray, Ben Lessy, Jerry Bergen, Val Setz, Gaudsmith Brothers, Cully Richards

Easter Parade
Metro-Goldwyn-Mayer
Released: 1948
Running time: 104 minutes
Produced by Arthur Freed
Directed by Charles Walters
Screenplay by Sidney Shelton, Frances Goodrich and Albert Hackett
Music and Lyrics by Irving Berlin
Costumes by Tom Keogh, supervised by Irene
Cast
Hannah Brown .... Judy Garland
Don Hewes .... Fred Astaire
Jonathan Harrow III .... Peter Lawford
Nadine Gale .... Ann Miller
Francois, the Headwaiter .... Jules Munshin
Mike, the Bartender .... Clinton Sundberg
Essie .... Jeni LeGon

Words and Music
Metro-Goldwyn-Mayer
Released: 1938
Running time: 119 minutes
Produced by Arthur Freed
Directed by Norman Taurog
Screenplay by Fred Finklehoffe, story by Guy Bolton and Jean Holloway
Music and Lyrics by Richard Rodgers and Lorenz Hart

Costumes by Helen Rose, Valles
Cast
Eddie Lorrison Anders .... Perry Como
Lorenz "Larry" Hart .... Mickey Rooney
Joyce Harmon .... Ann Sothern
Richard "Dick" Rodgers .... Tom Drake
Peggy Lorgan McNeil .... Betty Garrett
Dorothy Feiner .... anet Leigh
Herbert Fields .... Marshall Thompson
Mrs. Hart .... Jeanette Nolan
Ben Feiner, Jr. .... Richard Quine
Shoe Clerk .... Clinton Sundberg
Dr. Rodgers .... Harry Antrim
Mrs. Rodgers .... Ilka Gruning
Guest Appearances By: June Allyson, Cyd Charisse, Vera-Ellen, Edward Earle, Judy Garland, Lena Horne, Gene Kelly, Emory Parnell, Helen Spring, Mel Tormé, Dee Turnell, the Blackburn Twins
Featuring Judy Garland singing "Johnny One Note," and with Mickey Rooney "I Wish I Were in Love Again"

In the Good Old Summertime
Metro-Goldwyn-Mayer
Released: 1949
Running time: 104 minutes
Produced by Joe Pasternak
Directed by Robert Z. Leonard
Written for the screen by Albert Hackett, Frances Goodrich and Ivan Tors, from a screenplay by Samson Raphaelson, play by Miklos Laszlo
Musical Direction by Georgie Stoll
Costumes by Irene, Valles
Cast
Veronica Fisher .... Judy Garland
Andrew Delby Larkin .... Van Johnson
Otto Oberkugen .... S.Z. "Cuddles" Sakall
Nellie Burke .... Spring Byington
Rudy Hansen .... Clinton Sundberg
Hickey .... Buster Keaton
Louise Parkson .... Marcia Van Dyke
Aunt Addie .... Lillian Bronson

Summer Stock
Metro-Goldwyn-Mayer
Released: 1950
Running time: 110 minutes
Produced by Joe Pasternak
Directed by Charles Walters
Screenplay by George Wells and Sy Gomberg, based on a story by Sy Gomberg
Songs by Harry Warren and Mack Gordon, Saul Chaplin, Jack Brooks, Harold Arlen and Ted Koehler
Costumes by Walter Plunkett
Cast
Jane Falbury .... Judy Garland
Joe D. Ross .... Gene Kelly
Orville Wingait .... Eddie Bracken
Abigail Falbury .... Gloria DeHaven
Esmé .... Marjorie Main
Herb Blake .... Phil Silvers
Jasper G. Wingait .... Ray Collins
Sarah Higgins .... Nita Bieber
Artie .... Carleton Carpenter
Harrison I. Keath .... Hans Conried

A Star Is Born
Warner Bros.
A Transcona Enterprises Production
Released: 1954
Running time: 181 minutes
Produced by Sidney Luft
Directed by George Cukor, "Born in a Trunk" sequence directed by Richard Barstow
Screenplay by Moss Hart, based on a screenplay by Dorothy Parker, Alan Campbell and Robert Carson
Music and Lyrics by Harold Arlen and Ira Gershwin, "Born in a Trunk" by Leonard Gershe
Costumes by Irene Sharaff and Jean Louis
Cast
Esther Blodgett/Vicki Lester .... Judy Garland
Norman Maine .... James Mason
Matt Libby .... Jack Carson
Oliver Niles .... Charles Bickford

Danny McGuire .... Tom Noonan
with Irving Bacon, Amanda Blake, James Brown, Wilton Graff, Lucy Marlow,
Lotus Robb, Hazel Shermet, Grady Sutton
Judy Garland received an Academy Award nomination as Best Actress and
received a Golden Globe Award for Best Actress in a musical or comedy.

Pepe
Columbia Pictures
Released: 1960
Running time: 195 minutes
Produced and Directed by George Cukor
Screenplay by Dorothy Kingsley and Claude Binyon, based on a story by Leonard
   Spigelgass and Sonya Levien, from a play by L. Bush-Fekete
Music and Lyrics by Hans Wittstatt, Augustin Lara, Maria Teresa Lara, "The
   Faraway Part of Town" by André Previn and Dory Langdon
Gowns by Edith Head
Cast: Cantinflas, Dan Dailey, Shirley Jones, Carlos Montalban, Ernie Kovacs, Jay
North, Vicki Trickett, Matt Mattox, William Demarest, Michael Callan, Hank
Henry, Suzanne Lloyd, Lela Bliss, Ray Walker
Guest Stars: Maurice Chevalier, Bing Crosby, Richard Conte, Bobby Darin,
Sammy Davis, Jr., Jimmy Durante, Zsa Zsa Gabor, Greer Garson, Hedda Hopper,
Joey Bishop, Peter Lawford, Janet Leigh, Jack Lemmon, Kim Novack, Donna
Reed, Debbie Reynolds, Edward G. Robinson, Cesar Romero, Frank Sinatra, Ann
B. Davis, Billie Burke, Dean Martin, André Previn, Charles Coburn, Tony Curtis,
Carlos Rivas, and the voice of Judy Garland
Judy Garland is featured singing "The Faraway Part of Town."

Judgment at Nuremberg
United Artists
A Roxlom Production
Released: 1961
Running time: 190 minutes
Produced and Directed by Stanley Kramer
Screenplay by Abby Mann, based on his television play
Music by Ernest Gold
Costumes by Joe King
Cast
Judge Dan Haywood .... Spencer Tracy
Ernest Janning .... Bert Lancaster
Colonel Tad Lawson .... Richard Widmark
Madame Bertholt .... Marlene Dietrich
Hans Rolfe .... Maximilian Schell
Irene Hoffman .... Judy Garland
Rudolph Peterson .... Montgomery Clift
Captain Byers .... William Shatner
Senator Burkette .... Edward Binns
Judge Kenneth Norris .... Kenneth MacKenna
Emil Hahn .... Werner Klemperer
General Merrin .... Alan Baxter
Werner Lammpe .... Torben Meyer
with Ray Teal, Martin Brandt, Virginia Christine, Ben Wright, Joseph Bernard,
John Wengraf, Karl Swenson, Howard Caine, Otto Waldis, Olga Fabian, Sheila
Bromley, Bernard Kates, Jana Taylor, Paul Bush
Judy Garland was nominated for an Academy Award as Best Supporting Actress
and won the Cecil B. DeMille Golden Globe Award for her "contribution to the
entertainment industry throughout the years."

Gay Purr-ee
Warner Bros.
A UPA Production
Released: 1962
Running time: 86 minutes
Produced by Henry G. Saperstein
Directed by Abe Leviton
Screenplay by Dorothy and Chuck Jones
Music and Lyrics by Harold Arlen and E.Y. Harburg
Cast (Voices only): Judy Garland, Robert Goulet, Hermione Gingold, Red
Buttons, Morey Amsterdam, Paul Frees, Mel Blanc, Julie Bennett, Joan Gardner

A Child Is Waiting
United Artists
A Stanley Kramer Production
Released: 1963
Running time: 104 minutes
Produced by Stanley Kramer
Directed by John Cassavetes
Costumes by Howard Shoup
Cast
Dr. Matthew Clark .... Bert Lancaster

Kapralik art for *A Star Is Born.* **b.**

Jean Hansen .... Judy Garland
Sophie Widdicombe .... Gena Rowlands
Ted Widdicombe .... Steven Hill
Rueben Widdicombe .... Bruce Ritchey
Mattie .... Gloria McGehee
Goodman .... Paul Stewart
Douglas Benham .... Lawrence Tierney
Miss Fogarty .... Elizabeth Wilson
Miss Brown .... Barbara Pepper
Holland .... John Morley
Mrs. McDonald .... June Walker
Dr. Lombardi .... Marlo Gallo
Dr. Sack .... Frederick Draper

I Could Go On Singing
The Lonely Stage (U.K.)
United Artists
A Barbican Production
Released: 1963
Running time: 99 minutes
Produced by Stuart Millar and Lawrence Tirman
Directed by Ronald Neame
Screenplay by Mayo Simon, based on a story by Robert Dozier
Music by Mort Lindsey, "I Could Go On Singing" by Harold Arlen and E.Y.
   Harburg
Costumes by Edith Head
Cast
Jenny Bowman .... Judy Garland
David Donne .... Dirk Bogarde
George Kogan .... Jack Klugman
Matt .... Gregory Phillips
Ida .... Aline MacMahon
Miss Plimpton .... Pauline Jameson
Hospital surgeon .... Jeremy Burnham
with Russell Waters, Leon Cortez, Gerald Sim

Discography

Singles - 78 rpm

Listed chronologically by release date.

"Swing Mr. Charlie"
"Stompin' at the Savoy"
The Bob Crosby Orchestra - recorded June 12, 1936
Decca 848
Brunswick (U.K.) 02267

"Everybody Sing"
The Georgie Stoll Orchestra - recorded August 30, 1937
"When Two Love Each Other" (no vocal)
The Henry King Orchestra
Decca 13

"All God's Chillun Got Rhythm"
"Everybody Sing"
The Georgie Stoll Orchestra - recorded August 30, 1937
Decca 1432

"Dear Mr. Gable: You Made Me Love You"
"You Can't Have Everything"
The Harry Sosnick Orchestra - recorded September 24, 1937
Decca 1463

"Cry, Baby, Cry"
"Sleep My Baby Sleep"
The Harry Sosnick Orchestra - recorded April 24, 1938
Decca 1796

"It Never Rains But What It Pours"
"Ten Pins in the Sky"
The Harry Sosnick Orchestra - recorded August 21, 1938
Decca 2017
Brunswick (U.K.) 02656

"Over the Rainbow"
"The Jitterbug"
The Victor Young Orchestra - recorded September 28, 1939
Decca 2672
Decca 23962

"Oceans Apart"
"Figaro"
The Victor Young Orchestra - recorded October 16, 1939
Decca 2873
Brunswick (U.K.) 02953

"Zing! Went the Strings of My Heart"
"I'm Just Wild About Harry"
The Victor Young Orchestra - recorded July 29, 1939
Brunswick (U.K.) 02969

"Embraceable You"
"Swanee"
The Victor Young Orchestra - recorded October 16, 1939
Decca 2881

"Friendship" (with Johnny Mercer)
"Wearing of the Green"
The Bobby Sherwood Orchestra - recorded April 10 & 15, 1940
Decca 3165

"(Can This Be) The End of the Rainbow?"
"Wearing of the Green"
The Bobby Sherwood Orchestra - recorded June 10, April 15, 1940
Brunswick (U.K.) 03172

"Buds Won't Bud"
"I'm Nobody's Baby"
The Bobby Sherwood Orchestra - recorded June 10, 1940
Decca 3174

"(Can This Be) The End of the Rainbow?"
The Bobby Sherwood Orchestra - recorded June 10, 1940
"(Can This Be) The End of the Rainbow?" (no vocal)
The Woody Herman Orchestra
Decca 3231

"Our Love Affair"
"I'm Always Chasing Rainbows"
The David Rose Orchestra - recorded December 18, 1940
Decca 3593

"It's a Great Day for the Irish"
"A Pretty Girl Milking Her Cow"
The David Rose Orchestra - recorded December 18, 1940
Decca 3604
Decca 25043

"The Birthday of a King"
"Star of the East"
The David Rose Orchestra - recorded July 20, 1941
Decca 4050
Decca 23658

"How About You"
"F.D.R. Jones"
The David Rose Orchestra - recorded October 24, 1941
Decca 4072

"Blues in the Night"
The David Rose Orchestra - recorded October 24, 1941
"(Can This Be) The End of the Rainbow?"
The Bobby Sherwood Orchestra - recorded June 10, 1940
Decca 4081

"In-Between"
"Sweet Sixteen"
The Victor Young Orchestra - recorded July 28, 1939
Decca 15045
Decca 29233
Decca 40219

"Poor You"
"Last Call For Love"
The David Rose Orchestra - recorded April 3, 1942
Decca 18320

"For Me and My Gal" (with Gene Kelly)
"When You Wore a Tulip" (with Gene Kelly)
The David Rose Orchestra - recorded July 26, 1942
Decca 18480
Decca 25115
Brunswick (U.K.) 03432

"I Never Knew"
"On the Sunny Side of the Street"
The David Rose Orchestra - recorded July 26, April 3, 1942
Decca 18524

"That Old Black Magic"
"Poor Little Rich Girl"
The David Rose Orchestra - recorded March 3, 1942
Decca 18540

"Zing! Went the Strings of My Heart"
"Fascinatin' Rhythm"
The Victor Young Orchestra - recorded July 29, 1939
Decca 18543

"No Love, No Nothin'"
"A Journey to a Star"
The Georgie Stoll Orchestra - recorded December 22, 1943
Decca 18584
Brunswick (U.K.) 03515

"Embraceable You"
"Could You Use Me?" (with Mickey Rooney)
The Georgie Stoll Orchestra - recorded November 4, 1943
Decca 23308

"But Not For Me"
"Treat Me Rough" - Mickey Rooney
The Georgie Stoll Orchestra - recorded November 4, 1943
Decca 23309

"Bidin' My Time"
"I Got Rhythm"
The Georgie Stoll Orchestra - recorded November 2, 1943
Decca 23310

"Meet Me in St. Louis, Louis"
"Skip to My Lou"
The Georgie Stoll Orchestra - recorded April 24, 1944
Decca 23360

"The Trolley Song"
"Boys and Girls Like You and Me"
The Georgie Stoll Orchestra - recorded April 21, 1944
Decca 23361

"Have Yourself a Merry Little Christmas"
"The Boy Next Door"
The Georgie Stoll Orchestra - recorded April 20, 1944
Decca 23362

"The Boy Next Door"
"The Trolley Song"
The Georgie Stoll Orchestra - recorded April 20 & 21, 1944
Brunswick (U.K.) 03558

"This Heart of Mine"
"Love"
The Victor Young Orchestra - recorded January 26, 1945
Decca 18660
Brunswick (U.K.) 03623

"Yah-Ta-Ta, Yah-Ta-Ta" (with Bing Crosby)
"You've Got Me Where You Want Me" (with Bing Crosby)
The Joseph Lilley Orchestra - recorded March 9, 1945
Decca 23410

"On the Atchison, Topeka and the Santa Fe"
"If I Had You" (with The Merry Macs)
The Lyn Murray Orchestra - recorded May 17, July 7, 1945
Decca 23436

"It's a Great Big World" (with Betty Russell & Virginia O'Brien)
"The Wild, Wild West" - Virginia O'Brien
The Lennie Hayton Orchestra - recorded September 2, 1945
Decca 23460

"Smilin' Through"
"You'll Never Walk Alone"
The Lyn Murray Orchestra - recorded July 10, 1945
Decca 23539

"For You, For Me, For Evermore" (with Dick Haymes)
"Aren't You Kinda Glad We Did?" (with Dick Haymes)
The Gordon Jenkins Orchestra - recorded September 11, 1946
Decca 23687

"Changing My Tune"
The Gorgon Jenkins Orchestra - recorded September 11, 1946
"Love" The Victor Young Orchestra - recorded January 26, 1945
Decca 23688

"There Is No Breeze"
"Don't Tell Me That Story"
The Gordon Jenkins Orchestra - recorded October 1, 1946
Decca 23746

"Connecticut" (with Bing Crosby)
"Mine" (with Bing Crosby)
The Joseph Lilley Orchestra - recorded March 9, 1945
Decca 23804

"I Wish I Were in Love Again"
"Nothing But You"
The Goodwin & Griffen Twin Pianos - recorded January 15, 1947
Decca 24469

"Dear Mr. Gable: You Made Me Love You"
"Sleep, My Baby Sleep"
The Harry Sosnick Orchestra - recorded September 24, 1937, April 24, 1938
Decca 25393

"Dear Mr. Gable: You Made Me Love You"
The Harry Sosnick Orchestra - recorded September 24, 1937
"Over the Rainbow"
The Victor Young Orchestra - recorded September 28, 1939
Decca 25493

"On the Atchison, Topeka and the Santa Fe"
"In the Valley (Where the Evenin' Sun Goes Down)"
The Lennie Hayton Orchestra - recorded September 2, 1945
Decca 23438

"Wait and See" - Kenny Baker
"Round and Round"
The Lennie Hayton Orchestra - recorded September 2, 1945
Decca 23459

"The Trolley Song"
"Meet Me in St. Louis, Louis"
The Georgie Stoll Orchestra - recorded April 21, 1944
Decca 25494

"Mine" (with Bing Crosby)
"You've Got Me Where You Want Me" (with Bing Crosby)
The Joseph Lilley Orchestra - recorded March 9, 1945
Decca 28210

"Over The Rainbow"
"I May Be Wrong, But I Think You're Wonderful"
The Tommy Dorsey Orchestra - recorded 1944
V-Disc 335-A
Navy V-Disc 159-A

"Look for the Silver Lining"
"Life Upon the Wicked Stage" - Virginia O'Brien
The Lennie Hayton Orchestra - recorded 1946
MGM 30002

"Who?"
"Can't Help Lovin' Dat Man" - Lena Horne
The Lennie Hayton Orchestra - recorded 1946
MGM 30003

"Be a Clown" (with Gene Kelly)
"Pirate Ballet" (no vocal)
The Lennie Hayton Orchestra - recorded 1948
MGM 30097

"Love of My Life"
"You Can Do No Wrong"
The Lennie Hayton Orchestra - recorded 1948
MGM 30098

"Mack the Black"
"Nina" - Gene Kelly
The Lennie Hayton Orchestra - recorded 1948
MGM 30099

"Johnny One Note"
"I Wish I Were in Love Again" (with Mickey Rooney)
The Lennie Hayton Orchestra - recorded 1938
MGM 30172

"Easter Parade" (with Fred Astaire)
"A Fella With an Umbrella" (with Peter Lawford)
Johnny Green and the MGM Orchestra - recorded 1948
MGM 30185

"A Couple of Swells" (with Fred Astaire)
Medley: (with Fred Astaire)
    "I Love Piano"
    "Snooky Ookums"
    "When the Midnight Choo-Choo Leaves For Alabam"
Johnny Green and the MGM Orchestra - recorded 1948
MGM 30186

"Better Luck Next Time"
"It Only Happens When I Dance With You" - Fred Astaire
Johnny Green and the MGM Orchestra - recorded 1948
MGM 30187

"Who?"
"Look For the Silver Lining"

The Lennie Hayton Orchestra - recorded 1946
MGM 30431

"Put Your Arms Around Me Honey"
"Meet Me Tonight in Dreamland"
The Georgie Stoll Orchestra - recorded 1949
MGM 30205
MGM 50025

"Play that Barbershop Chord"
"I Don't Care"
The Georgie Stoll Orchestra - recorded 1949
MGM 30206
MGM 50026

"Merry Christmas"
"The Georgie Stoll Orchestra - recorded 1949
"Look For the Silver Lining"
The Lennie Hayton Orchestra - recorded 1946
MGM 30212

"Happy Harvest"
"If You Feel Like Singing, Sing"
Johnny Green and the MGM Orchestra - recorded 1950
MGM 30251

"Friendly Star"
"Get Happy"
Johnny Green and the MGM Orchestra - recorded 1950
MGM 30254

"Get Happy"
Johnny Green and the MGM Orchestra - recorded 1950
"Johnny One Note"
The Lennie Hayton Orchestra - recorded 1948
MGM 30429

"Put You Arms Around Me Honey"
The Georgie Stoll Orchestra - recorded 1949
"Love of My Life"
The Lennie Hayton Orchestra - recorded 1948
MGM 30430

"Last Night When We Were Young"
"Play That Barbershop Chord"
The Georgie Stoll Orchestra - recorded 1949
MGM 30432

"The Trolley Song"
The Georgie Stoll Orchestra - recorded 1944
"Cocktails for Two" - Tommy Dorsey
The Tommy Dorsey Orchestra - recorded 1946
Vouge Picture Records

"Send My Baby Back To Me"
"Without a Memory"

The Paul Weston Orchestra - recorded April 3, 1953
Columbia 40010
Columbia Canadian Records 2204

"Go Home, Joe"
"Heartbroken"
The Ray Heindorf Orchestra - recorded 1953
Columbia 40023
Columbia Canadian Records 2237

"The Man That Got Away"
"Here's What I'm Here For"
The Ray Heindorf Orchestra - recorded 1954
Columbia 40270

"Gotta Have Me Go With You"
"Lose That Long Face"
The Ray Heindorf Orchestra - recorded 1954
Columbia 8005

"The Man That Got Away"
"Someone at Last"
The Ray Heindorf Orchestra - recorded 1954
Columbia 8006

"Someone at Last"
"Born in a Trunk" - Medley
The Ray Heindorf Orchestra - recorded 1954
Columbia 8007

"It's a New World"
"Born in a Trunk" - Medley
The Ray Heindorf Orchestra - recorded 1954
Columbia 8008

"Here's What I'm Here For"
"Born in a Trunk" - Medley
The Ray Heindorf Orchestra - recorded 1954
Columbia 8009

126

Albums - 78 rpm

Listed chronologically by release date.

The Wizard of Oz
Decca A-74
Decca A-588

"Over the Rainbow"
"The Jitterbug"

Munchkinland - Part 1
Munchkinland - Part 2

"If I Only Had a Brain" - the Ken Darby Singers
"If I Only Had a Heart" - the Ken Darby Singers

"The Merry Old Land of Oz" - the Ken Darby Singers
"We're Off To See The Wizard" - the Ken Darby Singers

The Judy Garland Souvenir Album
Decca A-76

"Dear Mr. Gable: You Made Me Love You"
"You Can't Have Everything"

"Figaro"
"Oceans Apart"

"In-Between"
"Sweet Sixteen"

George Gershwin Songs, Volume Two
Decca A-97

"Swanee"
"Embraceable You"

(incomplete listing)

Christmas Candle
Decca A-347

"Birthday of a King"
"Star of the East"

(incomplete listing)

The Judy Garland Second Souvenir Album
Decca A-349

"For Me and My Gal" (with Gene Kelly)
"When You Wore a Tulip" (with Gene Kelly)

"That Old Black Magic"
"Poor Little Rich Girl"

"Zing! Went the Strings of My Heart"
"Fascinatin' Rhythm"

"On the Sunny Side of the Street"
"I Never Knew"

Meet Me in St. Louis
Decca A-380

"Meet Me in St. Louis, Louis"
"Skip to My Lou"

"The Trolley Song"
"Boys and Girls Like You and Me"

"Have Yourself a Merry Little Christmas"
"The Boy Next Door"

Girl Crazy
Decca A-362

"Embraceable You"
"Could You Use Me?" (with Mickey Rooney)

"But Not For Me"
"Treat Me Rough" - Mickey Rooney

"Bidin' My Time"
"I Got Rhythm"

The Harvey Girls
Decca A-388

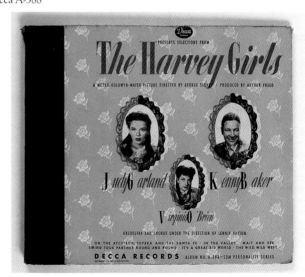

"On the Atchison, Topeka and the Santa Fe"
"In the Valley (Where the Evenin' Sun Goes Down)"

"Round and Round"
"Wait and See" - Kenny Baker

"It's a Great Big World" (with Betty Russell and Virginia O'Brien)
"The Wild, Wild West" - Virginia O'Bri"If I Had You" (with the Merry Macs

Christmastime
Decca A-488

"Birthday of a King"
"Star of the East"

(incomplete listing)

Bing Crosby Sings (with Judy Garland, Mary Martin, and Johnny Mercer)
Decca A-631

"Yah-Ta-Ta, Yah-Ta-Ta" (with Bing Crosby)
"You've Got Me Where You Want Me" (with Bing Crosby)

(incomplete listing)

The Judy Garland Third Souvenir Album
Decca A-671

"On the Sunny Side of the Street"
"I Never Knew"

"That Old Black Magic"
"Poor Little Rich Girl"

"Zing! Went the Strings of My Heart"
"Fascinatin' Rhythm"

"This Heart of Mine"
"Love"

Easter Parade
MGM-40

"Easter Parade" (with Fred Astaire)
"A Fella With an Umbrella" (with Peter Lawford)

"A Couple of Swells" (with Fred Astarie)
"Medley: (with Fred Astaire)
    "I Love Piano"
    "Snooky Ookums"
    "When the Midnight Choo-Choo Leaves For Alabam"
"Better Luck Next Time"
"It Only Happens When I Dance You" (with Fred Astaire)

Judy Garland Sings
Decca A-682

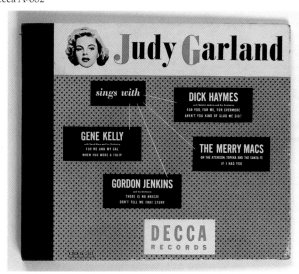

"If I Had You" (With the Merry Macs)
"On the Atchison, Topeka and the Santa Fe" (with the Merry Macs)

"Aren't You Kinda Glad We Did?" (with Dick Haymes)
"For You, For Me, For Evermore" (with Dick Haymes)

"Don't Tell Me That Story"
"There Is No Breeze"

"For Me and My Gal" (with Gene Kelly)
"When You Wore a Tulip" (with Gene Kelly)

Judy at the Palace
Decca A-899

"For Me and My Gal" (with Gene Kelly)
"When You Wore a Tulip" (with Gene Kelly)

"Dear Mr. Gable: You Made Me Love You"
"Over the Rainbow"

"The Trolley Song"
"Meet Me in St. Louis, Louis"

"In-Between"
"Sweet Sixteen"

Till the Clouds Roll By
MGM M-1

"Till the Clouds Roll By" (no vocal)
"Who Cares If My Boat Goes Upstream?"/"Make Believe"
Kathryn Grayson and Tony Martin

"Look For the Silver Lining" - Judy Garland
"Life Upon the Wicked Stage" - Virginia O'Brien

"Can't Help Lovin' Dat Man" - Lena Horne
"Who?" - Judy Garland

"Leave It To Jane"/"Cleopatterer" - June Allyson
"Ol' Man River" - Caleb Peterson

The Pirate
MGM - 21

Till the Clouds Roll By
MGM M-1

"Till the Clouds Roll By" (no vocal)
"Who Cares If My Boat Goes Upstream?"/"Make Believe" - Kathryn Grayson

"Be a Clown" (with Gene Kelly)
"Pirate Ballet" (no vocal)

Words and Music
MGM-37

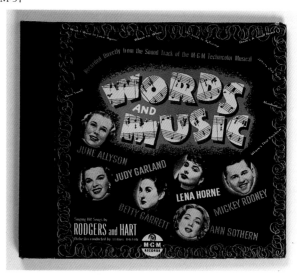

"Manhattan" - Mickey Rooney
"Thou Swell" - June Allyson

"The Lady Is a Tramp" - Lena Horne
"Where Or When" - Lena Horne

"I Wish I Were in Love Again" - Judy Garland and Mickey Rooney
"Johnny One Note" - Judy Garland

"There's a Small Hotel" - Betty Garrett
"Where's That Rainbow" - Ann Sothern

MGM's Silver Anniversary
MGM-42

"Jealousy" - Kathryn Grayson
"Can't Help Lovin' Dat Man" - Lena Horne

"French Lesson" - June Allyson and Peter Lawford
"Goodnight Sweetheart" - Van Johnson

"Love of My Life" - Judy Garland
"Nina" - Gene Kelly

"I'm the Guy Who Found the Lost Chord" - Jimmy Durante
"Ok'l Baby Dok'l" - Betty Garrett

In the Good Old Summertime
MGM L-11

"Put Your Arms Around Me Honey"
"Meet Me Tonight in Dreamland"

"Play That Barbershop Chord"
"I Don't Care"

Judy Garland Sings
MGM 82

"Who?"
"Get Happy"

"Love of My Life"
"Johnny One Note"

"Look For the Silver Lining"
"Play That Barber Shop Chord"

"Last Night When We Were Young"
"Put Your Arms Around Me Honey"

Summer Stock
MGM M-54

"Happy Harvest"
"If You Feel Like Singing, Sing"

"Friendly Star"
"Get Happy"

A Star Is Born
Columbia BM-1201

"Gotta Have Me Go With You"
"Lose That Long Face"

"The Man That Got Away"
"Someone at Last" - Part I

"Born in a Trunk" - Part I
"Someone at Last" - Part II

"Born in a Trunk" - Part II
"It's a New World"

"Born in a Trunk" - Part III
"Here's What I'm Here For"

Singles - 45 rpm

Listed chronologically by release date.

"Smilin' Through"
"You'll Never Walk Alone"
The Lyn Murray Orchestra - recorded July 10, 1945
Decca 9-23539

"The Birthday of a King"
"Star of the East"
The David Rose Orchestra - recorded July 20, 1941
Decca 9-23658

"Over the Rainbow"
"The Jitterbug"
The Victor Young Orchestra - recorded September 28, 1939
Decca 9-23961

"It's a Great Day for the Irish"
"A Pretty Girl Milking Her Cow"
The David Rose Orchestra - recorded December 18, 1940
Decca 9-25043

"For Me and My Gal" (with Gene Kelly)
"When You Wore a Tulip" (with Gene Kelly)
The David Rose Orchestra - recorded July 26, 1942

"Dear Mr. Gable: You Made Me Love You"
The Harry Sosnick Orchestra - recorded September 24, 1937
"Over the Rainbow"
The Victor Young Orchestra - recorded September 28, 1939
Decca 9-25493

"The Trolley Song"
"Meet Me in St. Louis, Louis"
The Georgie Stoll Orchestra - recorded April 24, 1944
Decca 9-25494

"Mine" (with Bing Crosby)
"You've Got Me Where You Want Me" (with Bing Crosby)
The Joseph Lilley Orchestra - recorded 1945
Decca 9-28210

"Have Yourself a Merry Little Christmas"
The Georgie Stoll Orchestra - recorded April 24, 1944
"You'll Never Walk Alone"
The Lyn Murray Orchestra - recorded July 10, 1945
Decca 9-29295

"The Boy Next Door"
The Georgie Stoll Orchestra - recorded April 24, 1944
"Smilin' Through"
The Lyn Murray Orchestra - recorded July 10, 1945
Decca 9-29296

"In-Between"
"Sweet Sixteen"
The Victor Young Orchestra - recorded July 28, 1939
Decca 9-40219

"Look for the Silver lining"
"Who?"
The Lennie Hayton Orchestra - recorded 1946
MGM 30212

"Get Happy"
"Friendly Star"
Johnny Green and the MGM Orchestra - recorded 1950
MGM30254

"Zing! Went the Strings of My Heart"
"Rock-a-Bye Your Baby With a Dixie Melody"
The Mort Lindsey Orchestra - recorded 1961
Capital 4624

"Once in a Lifetime"
"Sweet Danger"
The Mort Lindsey Orchestra - recorded 162
Capital 4656

"Hello, Bluebird"
"I Could Go On Singing"
The Mort Lindsey Orchestra -recorded 1963
Capital 4938

"Hello, Dolly!" (with Liza Minnelli)
"He's Got the Whole World in His Hands"
The Harry Robinson Orchestra - recorded 1964
Capital 5497

"Maybe I'll Come Back"
The Nelson Riddle Orchestra - recorded 1956
"Over the Rainbow"
The Jack Cathcart Orchestra - recorded 1955
Capital 6128

"San Francisco"
"Chicago"
The Mort Lindsey Orchestra - recorded 1961
Capital 6125

"The Man That Got Away"
The Mort Lindsey Orchestra - recorded 1961
"April Showers"
The Nelson Riddle Orchestra - recorded 1956
Capital 6126

"Come Rain or Come Shine"
"Rock-a-Bye Your Baby With a Dixie Melody"
The Mort Lindsey Orchestra - recorded 1961
Capital 6127

"Swanee"
"That's Entertainment"
The Mort Lindsey Orchestra - recorded 1961
Capital 6129

"Maggie, Maggie May"
"There's Only One Union"
"The Land of Promises"
"It's Yourself"
Capital EAP 1-20630

"Lucky Day"
"Dirty Hands, Dirty Face"
"Last Night When We Were Young"
Capital EAP 1-734

"It's Lovely to Be Back Again in London"
"By Myself"
Capital EMI (U.K.) 45-CL-14791

"Little Drops of Rain"
"Paris Is a Lonely Town"
The Mort Lindsey Orchestra - recorded 1962
Warner Bros. 5310

"(Dear Mr. Gable) You Made Me Love You"
The Georgie Stoll Orchestra - recorded September 24, 1937
"Over the Rainbow"
The Victor Young Orchestra - recorded September 28, 1939
MCA 60066

Albums - 33 1/3 rpm

Listed chronologically by release date.

Judy Garland
MGM E 3149
MGM Metro M/MS 505

"Last Night When We Were Young"
"Play That Barber Shorp Chord"
"Who?"
"Look For the Silver Lining"
"Love of My Life"

"Get Happy"
"Johnny One Note"
"Better Luck Next Time"
"If You Feel Like Singing, Sing"
"I Don't Care"
"Meet Me Tonight In Dreamland"

The Magic of Judy Garland
Decca DL 4199
Ace of Hearts AH 128

"I Never Knew"
"On the Sunny Side of the Street"
"F.D.R. Jones"
"But Not For Me"
"I'm Always Chasing Rainbows"
"Our Love Affair"

"That Old Black Magic"
"A Pretty Girl Milking Her Cow"
"On the Atchison, Topeka and the Santa Fe"
"Embraceable You"
"Zing! Went the Strings of My Heart"
"I'm Nobody's Baby"

Judy Garland, Greatest Performances
Decca DL 8190

"Dear Mr. Gable: You Made Me Love You"
"Over the Rainbow"
"How About You?"
"In-Between"
"For Me and My Gal"
"Love"

"The Trolley Song"
"Meet Me in St. Louis, Louis"
"Poor Little Rich Girl"
"Sweet Sixteen"
"When You Wore a Tulip" (with Gene Kelly)
"You'll Never Walk Alone"

Miss Show Business
Capital W-676
Capital EDM 2-676 (45 rpm)
Capital DW-676
Capital/Applause APCL 3322

Judy
Capital T-734
Capital DT-734
Capital EAP 734-1/2/3 (45 rpm)
Capital (U.K.) LCT-6121

"This Is the Time of the Evening"
"While We're Young"
Medley:
    "You Made Me Love You"
    "For Me and My Gal"
    "The Boy Next Door"
    "The Trolley Song"
"A Pretty Girl Milking Her Cow"
"Rock-a-Bye Your Baby With a Dixie Melody"
"Happiness Is Just a Thing Called Joe"

Medley: Judy at the Palace
    "Shine On, Harvest Moon"
    "My Man"
    "Some of These Days"
    "I Don't Care"
"Carolina in the Morning"
"Danny Boy"
"After You've Gone"
"Over the Rainbow"

"Come Rain or Come Shine"
"Just Imagine"
"I Feel a Song Coming On"
"Last Night When We Were Young"
"Life Is Just a Bowl of Cherries"
"April Showers"

"I Will Come Back"
"Dirty Hands, Dirty Face"
"Lucky Day"
"Memories of You"
"Any Place I Hang My Hat Is Home"

Alone
Capital T-835
Capital DT-835
Capital EAP 835-1/2/3 (45 rpm)

"By Myself"
"Little Girl Blue"
"Me and My Shadow"
"Among My Souvenirs"
"I Get the Blues When It Rains"

"Mean to Me"
"How About Me?"
"Just a Memory"
"Blue Prelude"
"Happy New Year"

Judy in Love
Capital T-1036
Capital ST-1036
Capital EAP 1036-1/2/3 (45 rpm)

"Zing! Went the Strings of My Heart"
"I Can't Give You Anything But Love"
"This Is It"
"More Than You Know"
"I am Loved"

"I Hadn't Anyone Till You"
"I Concentrate on You"
"I'm Confessin'"
"Do I Love You?"
"Do It Again"
"Day In-Day Out"

The Letter
Capital S/TAO 1188
Our Love Letter (1963 re-issue)
Capital ST-1941

"Beautiful Trouble"
"Love in the Village"
"Charley's Blues"
"The Worst Kind of Man"
"That's All There Is, There Isn't Any More"

"Love in Central Park"
"The Red Balloon"
"The Fight"
"At the Stroke of Midnight"
"Come Back"

Judy! That's Entertainment
Capital T-1467
Capital ST-1467
Capital SLER-6528
Capital SM-11876

"That's Entertainment"
"Who Cares! (So Long As You Care For Me)"
"If I Love Again"
"Yes"
"Puttin' on the Ritz"

"Old Devil Moon"
"Down With Love"
"It Never Was You"
"Just You, Just Me"
"Alone Together"

The Garland Touch
Capital W1710

"I Happen to Like New York"
"Comes Once in a Lifetime"
Medley: Judy at the Palace
    "Shine On Harvest Moon"
    "Some of These Days"
    "My Man"
    "I Don't Care"

"Happiness Is Just a Thing Called Joe"
"Sweet Danger"
"You'll Never Walk Alone"
"Do I Love You?"
"More Than You'll Know"
"It's a Great Day For the Irish"

The Hits of Judy Garland
Capital SN-16175

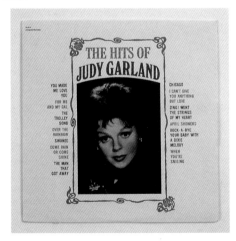

Medley:
    "You Made Me Love You"
    "For Me and My Gal"
    "The Trolley Song"
"Over the Rainbow"
"Swanee"
"Come Rain Or Come Shine"
"The Man That Got Away"

"Chicago"
"Zing! Went the Strings of My Heart"
"April Showers"
"Rock-a-Bye Your Baby With a Dixie Melody"
"When You're Smiling (the Whole World Smiles With You)"

Judy in London
Capital 94407
Capital SLB 8099

"Lucky Day"
Medley:
    "You Made Me Love You"
    "For Me and My Gal"
    "The Trolley Song"
"Happiness Is Just a Thing Called Joe"
"Rock-a-Bye Your Baby With a Dixie Melody"
"Stormy Weather"

"The Man That Got Away"
"San Francisco"
"I Can't Give You Anything But Love"
"Chicago"
"Do It Again"

"Over the Rainbow"
"After You've Gone"
"I Happen to Like New York"
"Why Was I Born?"
"You Go To My Head"

Medley: Judy at the Palace:
    "Shine On, Harvest Moon"
    "Some of These Days"
    "My Man"
    "I Don't Care"
"It's a Great Day For the Irish"
"Come Rain or Come Shine"
"Swanee"
"You'll Never Walk Alone"

Additional 33 1/3 rpm Albums

Listed alphabetically.

All of Judy
Telebrity 1228

Around the Christmas Tree (with various Decca artists)
Decca DL 9056

the beginning
DRG Records SL-5187

The Best of Judy Garland
Decca DXB 1-72
Decca DXSB 7172
Coral (U.K.) CP 54
MCA 24003
MCA MCL-1630

The Best of Judy Garland - The Capital Years
Capital EMS 1347

Born to Sing
MGM (U.K.) 134 (10")

Christmas With Judy Garland
Minerva MIN-LP-6JG-XST

Forever Judy
MGM PX-102

Girls and More Girls (with various MGM artists)
MGM L-70118
MGM Lion L-70118

Golden Memories of Judy Garland
Capital/Pair PDL 2-1030

The Great Garland Duets
Paragon 1001

The Great Garland Duets - Judy Garland
Broadcast Tributes BTRIB-0002

The Great MGM Stars - Judy Garland
MGM EMI LPMGM 29

The Hits of Judy Garland
Capital EMI VMP-1011

House Party (with various Decca artists)
Decca DL 4206

I Feel a Song Coming On
Capital/Pickwick PC-3053

If You Feel Like Singing, Sing
MGM X-268 (10")

The Immortal Judy Garland
Longines Symphonette SY 5217 - 5221

Judy
Radiant 711-0101
Audiofidelity AFE-3-5

Judy - All Alone
Tucker TLP-201
Meteor MFM-025

Judy and Her Partners in Rhythm and Rhyme
Startone ST-213

Judy at the Palace
Decca DL 6020 (10")
Decca ED 620
Brunswick (U.K.) LAT 8725

Judy Garland
Audiofidelity (picture disc) PD-311
Metronome KMLP-318

Judy Garland and Friends
Minerva MIN-6JG-FNJ

Judy Garland - Born in a Trunk, Stardom 1940 - 45
AEI 2109

Judy Garland - Born in a Trunk, Superstar 1945 - 50
AEI 2110

Judy Garland - By Myself
Sears SP-430

The Judy Garland Collection - 20 Great Hits
Dejavu DULP-2002

Judy Garland "Collector's Items"
Coral (U.K.) CP-53

Judy Garland - Collector's Items 1936 - 1945
Decca DEA 7-5
Coral (U.K.) CP 53,54
MCA 2-4046

Judy Garland - Concert
Trophy Records TR 7-2145

The Judy Garland Deluxe Set
Capital STCL 2988

Judy Garland - From MGM Classic Films, 1938 - 1950
MCA 25165

Judy Garland - From the Decca Vaults
MCA 907

Judy Garland, Great Performances
Decca DL 8190
Brunswick (U.K.) AH 11
Ace of Hearts (U.K.) AH 11

Judy Garland's Greatest Hits
Decca DL 75150

Judy Garland - Her Greatest Hits
Capital PTP-2010

Judy Garland in Song
MGM Metro M/MS 581

Judy Garland - Legendary Singers
Capital/Time Life SLGD-12

The Judy Garland Musical Scrapbook
Startone ST-208

Judy Garland - Over the Rainbow
Capital/Pickwick PC-3078
Phoenix PHX-311

Judy Garland Recital
Capital EMI 541-2604091

The Judy Garland Show
Minerva MIN-6JG-FST

Judy Garland Sings
MGM E-82 (10")

Judy Garland Star Eyes
Audiofidelity AFE-3-4

The Judy Garland Story - The Hollywood Years, Vol. II
MGM E-4005 P
MGM 2683005
MGM (U.K.) C-887

The Judy Garland Story - The Star Years
MGM E-3989 P
MGM 2354014
MGM (U.K.) C-886

Judy Garland - The ABC Collection
ABC ABCS-620

Judy Garland - The Golden Archive Series
MGM GAS-113

Judy Garland - The Golden Years at MGM
MGM SDP1-2

Judy Garland - The Original Recordings
MCA MCM-5023

Judy Garland - Twelve Hits
Oxford OX-3030

Judy Garland - 20 Hits of a Legend
Nostalgia (picture disc) 22004

Judy Garland, Volume II
Decca ED 2050

Judy in Hollywood
Radiant 711-0102

Judy! Judy! Judy!
Startone ST-224

Judy's Portrait in Song
Radiant 711-0106

Judy the Legend
Radiant 711-0103

Just for Openers
Capital W/DW 2062
Capital M-12034

The Legendary Judy Garland
Capital/Pair PDL 2-1127

The Legendary Judy Garland - I Could Go On Singing
Capital MLM SLC 57051

The Magic of Judy Garland
Decca DL4199

Magnificent Moments from MGM Movies (with various MGM artists)
MGM E-4017

Merry Christmas (with various MGM artists)
MGM M-169

Merry Christmas - Judy Garland
Audiofidelity HDY-1952

The MGM 30th Anniversary Album (with various MGM artists)
MGM E 3118
MGM X 240 (45 rpm)

Miss Show Biz
Brunswick (U.K.) AH 48

More Stars in Stereo (with various Capital artists)
Capital SW 1162

More Than a Memory- the Uncollected Judy Garland
Stanyon 10095

A Musical Autobiography of Bing
Decca DL 8075
Decca ED 1700 (45 rpm)
Brunswick (U.K.) LAT 8054

Open House (with various Decca artists)
Decca DL 4205

Original Hit Performances - Into the 40s (with various Decca artists)
Decca DL-4001

Original Hit Performances - The 40s (with various Decca artists)
Decca DL-4002

Original Hit Performances-The Late 30s (with various Decca artists)
Decca DL-4000

Over the Rainbow - Judy Garland
MCA MFP-50555
Springboard SPB-4054

The Picks of Judy
CSP P18051

Showstoppers (with various Capital artists)
Capital SL-6524

The Silver Screen (with various artists)
Harmony H-305449

Styled Just For You (with various Capital artists)
Capital ST 1036

That's Entertainment (with various Capital artists)
Capital SLER-06528

Those Memory Years (with various Decca artists)
Decca TMY 1-C

3 Billion Millionaires (with various artists)
United Artists UXS 54
United Artists UXL 4

The Unforgettable Judy Garland
Radiant 711-0105

The Very Best of Irving Berlin (with various MGM artists)
MGM E/SE-4240

The Very Best of Jerome Kern (with various MGM artists)
MGM E/SE-4241

The Very Best of Judy Garland
MGM E/SE-4204

The Very Best of Motion Picture Musicals (with various MGM artists)
MGM E/SE-4171

The Very Best of Rodgers and Hart (with various MGM artists)
MGM E/SE-4238

What's New? vol. 1 (with various Capital artists)
Capital SN-1

The Young Judy Garland
MCA MCL-1731

Radio Broadcast Albums

Listed chronologically by release date.

Hollywood on the Air
Startone ST-201

"Broadway Rhythm"
"Smiles"
"Over the Rainbow"
"Nobody"
"America"
"I May Be Wrong"
"I Don't Care"

"Pretty Baby" (with Al Jolson)
"For Me and My Gal" (with Bing Crosby)
"Who?"
"Embraceable You"
"Alexander's Ragtime Band"
"Wish You Were Here"
"A Pretty Girl Milking Her Cow"
"Carolina in the Morning"
"You Belong to Me"
"Rock-a-Bye Your Baby With a Dixie Melody"

Dick Tracy in B-Flat
Curtain Calls 100/1
Sandy Hook 2052
Scarce Rarities 5504

Overture
"Whose Dream Are You?" - Bing Crosby
"Who's That Knocking at My Door?" - Bing Crosby, Dinah Shore
"I Had a Friend, and I Had a Phone" - Dinah Shore
"I'm the Top" - Bob Hope
"A Wandering Actor I" - Frank Morgan
"Music Goes Round and Round" - Jimmy Durante
"Somewhere Over the Rainbow" - Judy Garland

"I'm Gonna Go For You" - Judy Garland, Bob Hope
"Whose Dream Are You?" (reprise) - Bing Crosby
"Apple Blossom Time" - The Andrew Sisters
"All the Things You Are" - Frank Sinatra, Bing Crosby
"Sunday, Monday and Always" - Bing Crosby, Bob Hope, Frank Sinatra
"The Trolley Song" - Cass Daley
Finale - Cast

Judy Garland on Radio
Radiola MR-1040

The Gulf Screen Show (with George Murphy)
The Bing Crosby Show (with Bing Crosby, Ken Carpenter)
The Kraft Music Hall (with Al Jolson)
Maxwell House Coffee Time
The General Electric Program (with Ken Carpenter, John Scott Trotter Orchestra, Rhythmaires, Ziggy Elman)

The Rare Early Broadcast Performances - Judy Garland
Starcast STCT-1001
Accessor Pro STCT-1001

"Broadway Rhythm"
"Smiles"
"Over the Rainbow"
"Nobody"
"America"
"I May Be Wrong"

"I Don't Care"
"Alexander's Ragtime Band"
"Pretty Baby"
"For Me and My Gal"
"Who?"
"Embraceable You"

Bing Crosby & Judy Garland "Mail Call"
Tandem LP-1903

"The Dixieland Band"
"I Love You" - Bing Crosby
"All The Things You Are" - Frank Sinatra
"You're the Top" - Bing Crosby, Frank Sinatra, Bob Hope
"Something to Remember You By" (with Bing Crosby)

"The Trolley Song"
"Love, Love, Love" - Bing Crosby
"Can Do, Will Do"
"Amor" - Bing Crosby
"The Groaner, The Canary and the Nose" (with Bing Crosby, Jimmy Durante)

Frances Ethel Gumm and Harry Lillis Crosby: Judy and Bing Together
Legend WM-1973

"Punchy and Judy" (with Bing Crosby)
"I Like You Just the Way You Are" (with Bing Crosby)
Medley: (with Bing Crosby)
    "Hello, My Baby, Hello, My Honey"
    "In My Merry Oldsmobile"
    "Call Me Up Some Rainy Afternoon"
    "Walking My Baby Back Home"
    "In My Merry Oldsmobile" (reprise)

"You Made Me Love You"
"How Could You Believe Me When I Said I Loved You When You Know
I've Been A Liar All My Life?" (with Bing Crosby)
"You're Just in Love"
Medley: (with Bing Crosby)
    "Tortured" - Bing Crosby
    "Boise, Idaho"
    "My , Blue Boy"
    "These Lush Moments"
"Mean to Me"
Medley: (with Bing Crosby)
    "Bon Voyage, Judy" - Bing Crosby
    "Limehouse Blues"
    "April in Paris"
    "Isle of Capri"

Judy Garland in *A Star Is Born* - Lux Radio Theatre
Radiola MR-1155

Lux Radio Theatre (no listing)

The Wit & Wonder of Judy Garland
DRG SL-5179

"Thanks For The Memories"
"Dardenella"
"Americana"
"People Will Say We're in Love"
"Dixieland Jazz"
"Long Ago and Far Away"
"Why Was I Born?"
"Lorna"

Television Broadcasts (no listing for side 2)

Additional Radio Broadcast Albums include:

Behind the Scenes at the Making of *The Wizard of Oz*
Jass 17

Bing, Bob and Judy
Totem 1000

Judy Garland in *A Star Is Born*
Radiola MR-1155

Meet Me in St. Louis - Lux Radio Theatre
Pelican 118

Merton of the Movies
Pelican 139

Philco Radio Time, vol. 1
Totem 1002

The Wizard of Oz - Lux Radio Theater
Sandy Hook MR-1109

Concert Albums

Listed chronologically by release date.

Judy at Carnegie Hall
Capital WBO-1569
Capital SWBO-1569
Capital EAP-1569 (45 rpm)
Capital SENC-9750 (vol. 2)
Capital SXA-1596 (45 rpm)

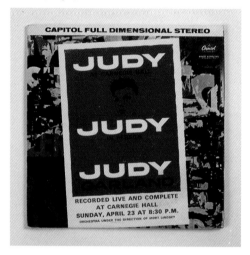

Overture
Medley:
    "It's Almost Like Being in Love"
    "This Can't Be Love"
"Do It Again"
"You Go to My Head"
"Alone Together"

"Who Cares?"
"Puttin' on the Ritz"
"How Long Has This Been Going On?"
"Just You, Just Me"
"San Francisco"
"I Can't Give You Anything But Love"
"That's Entertainment"

"Come Rain or Come Shine"
"You're Nearer"
"A Foggy Day"
"If Love Were All"
"Zing! Went the Strings of My Heart"
"Stormy Weather"

Medley:
    "You Made Me Love You"
    "For Me and My Gal"
    "The Trolley Song"
"Rock-a-Bye Your Baby With a Dixie Melody"
"Over the Rainbow"
"Swanee"
"After You've Gone"
"Chicago"

Judy Garland and Liza Minnelli - Live at the Palladium
Capital WBO-2295
Capital SWBO-2295
World Record Club (U.K.) ST-764/5
Capital EM-1249 (re-issue)
Capital ST-11191 (re-issue as shown)

Judy Garland at the Grove
Capital T-1118
Capital ST-1118
Capital 26-0007-1
EMI (U.K.) 260007

"Together (Wherever We Go)" (with Liza Minnelli)
"The Man That Got Away"
"Who's Sorry Now" - Liza Minnelli
Medley:
    "Hooray For Love" (with Liza Minnelli)
    "After You've Gone"
    "By Myself" - Liza Minnelli
    "'S Wonderful"
    "How About You?" (with Liza Minnelli)
    "Lover Come Back to Me" - Liza Minnelli
    "You and the Night and the Music"
    "It All Depends on You" (with Liza Minnelli)
"What Now, My Love?"

"Hello, Dolly!" (with Liza Minnelli)
"Gypsy in My Soul" - Liza Minnelli
"Swanee" (with Liza Minnelli)
"Over the Rainbow"
"When the Saints Go Marching In"/"Brotherhood of Man" (with Liza Minnelli)
"He's Got the Whole World in His Hands" (with Liza Minnelli)

Overture
"When You're Smiling"
"Zing! Went the Strings of My Heart"
"Purple People Eater"
Medley:
    "You Made Me Love You"
    "For Me and My Gal"
    "The Trolley Song"

"When the Sun Comes Out"
"Rock-a-Bye Your Baby With a Dixie Melody"
"Over the Rainbow"
"After You've Gone"
"A Pretty Girl Milking Her Cow"
"Swanee"

Judy Garland at Home at the Palace Opening Night
ABC 620
ABC S-620

Overture
"I Feel a Song Coming On"
Medley:
    "Almost Like Being in Love"
    "This Can't Be Love"
Medley:
    "You Made Me Love You"
    "For Me and My Gal"
    "The Trolley Song"
"What Now My Love?"

"Bob White" (with Lorna Luft)
"Jamboree Jones" (with Lorna Luft)
"Together" (with Lorna Luft, Joe Luft)
"Over the Rainbow" (Instrumental)
"Ol' Man River"
"That's Entertainment"
"I Loved Him, But He Didn't Love Me"
"Rock-a-Bye Your Baby With a Dixie Melody"
"Over the Rainbow" (Instrumental)

For Collectors Only
Paragon 1002

"Sail Away"
"Something's Coming"
"Just in Time"
"Get Me to the Church on Time"
"Never Will I Marry"
"Joey, Joey"

"Hey, Look Me Over"
"The Party's Over"
"Some People"
"Maggie, Maggie May"
"There's Only One Union"
"The Land of Promises"
"It's Yourself"

Judy-London 1969
Juno S-1000
Sunset (U.K.) 50196

"I Belong to London"
"Get Happy"
"The Man That Got Away"
"I'd Like to Hate Myself in the Morning"

"Just in Time"
Medley:
       "You Made Me Love You"
       "For Me and My Gal"
       "The Trolley Song"
"For Once in My Life"
"San Francisco"
"Over the Rainbow"

Judy Garland in Concert - San Francisco
Mark 56 632

Overture
"I Feel a Song Coming On"
Medley:
       "You Made Me Love You"
       "For Me and My Gal"
       "The Trolley Song"
"Do It Again"
"The Man That Got Away"
"Rock-a-Bye Your Baby With a Dixie Melody"

"I Can't Give You Anything But Love"
"Purple People Eater"
"Liza"

Listed alphabetically, additional concert albums include:

Judy Garland in Holland, vol. 2
Obligato GIH-610

Judy Garland in Holland, vol. 3
Obligato GIH-6100

**Judy Garland "Live" at the Palace, February 1952:
An Evening of Song, Dance and Conversation**
Classic International Theatermusic CIT-2001

Judy Garland - The Last Concert
Paragon 1003

The Long Last Hollywood Concert "The Rarest Garland Ever"
Obligato GIH 60

Motion Picture Soundtracks

Listed chronologically.

Pigskin Parade/Everybody Sing
Pilgrim 4000

"The Balboa" (with cast)
"The Texas Tornado"
"It's Love I'm After"

"Swing Mr. Mendelssohn, Swing"
"Down On Melody Farm"
"Why? Because" (with Fanny Brice)
"I Wanna Swing"

The Wizard Of Oz
MGM E3464
MGM X-3464 (45 rpm)
MGM ST-3464
MGM E-3996
MGM PX-104
MGM (U.K.) 2353044
MCA 30046
AH 121

"Over the Rainbow"
"Ding-Dong! The Witch is Dead" (with Billie Burke, the Munchkins)
"We're Off to See the Wizard" - the Munchkins

"If I Only Had a Brain" - Ray Bolger
"If I Only Had a Heart" - Jack Haley
"If I Only Had the Nerve" - Bert Lahr
"We're Off to See the Wizard" (reprise, with Ray Bolger, Jack Haley, Bert Lahr)
"You're Out of the Woods" - chorus
"The Merry Old Land of Oz" - chorus
"If I Were the King of the Forest" - Bert Lahr

Ziegfeld Girl
Classic International Filmusicals CIF-3006

Overture
"Laugh? I Thought I'd Split My Sides" (with Charles Winninger)
"You, Stepped Out of a Dream" - Tony Martin
"I'm Always Chasing Rainbows"

"Caribbean Love Song" - Tony Martin
"Minnie From Trinidad"
"Mr. Gallagher and Mr. Shean" - Charles Winninger, Al Shean
Finale:
"Ziegfeld Girls" (with chorus)
"You Gotta Pull Strings" (with chorus)
"We Must Have Music" (with Tony Martin)
"You Stepped Out of a Dream" (reprise) - Tony Martin
"You Never Looked So Beautiful Before" (with chorus)
End Titles

For Me and My Gal
Soundtrak STK-107

Babes on Broadway
MGM ML-101677
Curtain Call CC-100/6-7

Main Title
"Anything Can Happen in New York" - Mickey Rooney
"How About You?" (with Mickey Rooney)
"Hoe Down" (with Mickey Rooney)
"Chin Up! Cheerio! Carry On!"

Cyrano
"Mary (It's a Grand Old Name)"
"Daisy" - Mickey Rooney
"Rings On My Fingers"
Sarah Bernhart
"Yankee Doodle Boy" - Mickey Rooney
"Bombshell From Brazil" (with Mickey Rooney, Richard Quine,
      Ray McDonald, Virginia Weidler)
"Mama, Yo Quiero" - Mickey Rooney
"Blackout Over Broadway" (with cast)
"The Minstrel Show" (with Mickey Rooney)
"By the Light of the Silvery Moon" - Chorus
"F.D.R. Jones"
"Swanee River" - Instrumental
"Waitin' for the Robert E. Lee"
"Babes on Broadway" (with cast)

Overture
"Oh, Johnny" (Gene Kelly dance sequence)
"Oh, You Beautiful Doll" - Lucille Norman, George Murphy
"Don't Leave Me Daddy"
"Oh, You Beautiful Doll" - George Murphy
"By the Beautiful Sea" (with George Murphy)
"For Me and My Gal" (with Gene Kelly)
"When You Wore a Tulip" (with Gene Kelly)
"Do I Love You?" - Marta Eggerth

"After You've Gone"
"Tell Me" - Lucille Norman
"Till We Meet Again" - Lucille Norman
"We Don't Want the Bacon" - Ben Lessey
"Ballin' the Jack" (with Gene Kelly)
"What Are You Gonna Do For Uncle Sammy?" - Ben Blue
"How You Gonna Keep Them Down on the Farm?"
Medley:
      "Where Do We Go From Here?"
      "It's a Long Way to Tipperary"
      "Over There"
      "Goodbye Broadway, Hello France" - chorus
      "Smiles"
      "Oh Frenchy" - Gene Kelly, Ben Blue
      "Pack Up Your Troubles"
"When Johnny Comes Marching Home"
"For Me and My Gal" - closing theme

Presenting Lily Mars
Soundtrak STK-117

Opening, Act One
Macbeth Scene
Act One Continued
"Tom, Tom, the Piper's Son"
Act Two
"Every Little Movement" (with Connie Gilchrist)

"When I Look at You"
"Baby, Think of Me" - Bob Crosby Orchestra
"When I Look at You" (comedy version)
Finale Medley:
      "Where There's Music" (with chorus)
      "Three O'Clock in the Morning" (with chorus)
      "Broadway Rhythm"

Meet Me in St. Louis/The Harvey Girls
Decca DL-8498
AEI 3101

"Meet Me in St. Louis, Louis"
"Skip to My Lou" (with cast)
"The Trolley Song"
"Boys and Girls Like You and Me"
"Have Yourself a Merry Little Christmas"
"The Boy Next Door"

"On the Atchison, Topeka and the Santa Fe"
"In the Valley (Where the Even' Sun Goes Down)"
"Wait and See" - Kenny Baker
"Swing Your Partner Round and Round" (with cast and chorus)
"It's a Great Big World" (with Virginia O'Brien, Betty Russell)
"The Wild, Wild West" - Virginia O'Brien

Annie Get Your Gun
MGM E-3001
Hollywood Soundstage 2302
Sandy Hook SH-2053
Our Fed ACYC-100
Dr. Green's Wax Works AGYG 100

"You Can't Get a Man With a Gun"
"Doin' What Comes Naturally"
"They Say It's Wonderful" (with Howard Keel)
"Anything You Can Do" (with Howard Keel)
"Let's Go West Again"
"I'm an Indian Too"

"I've Got the Sun in the Morning"
"The Girl That I Marry" - Howard Keel
"My Defenses Are Down" - Howard Keel
"The Girl That I Marry" (reprise) - Howard Keel
"There's No Business Like Show business"

Till the Clouds Roll By
MGM X-1 (45 rpm)
MGM E-501
MGM E-3231
MGM E-3779
MGM SES-45-ST
Metro M-578
MCA 25000
Sandy Hook SH-2080

"Till the Clouds Roll By" - Lennie Hayton and the MGM orchestra
"Look for the Silver Lining"
"Can't Help Lovin' Dat Man" - Lena Horne
"Leave it to Jane/Cleopatterer - June Allyson

"Make Believe"/"Who Cares If My Boat Goes Upstream" - Kathryn Grayson, Tony Martin
"Life Upon the Wicked Stage" - Virginia O'Brien
"Who?"
"Ol' Man River" - Caleb Peterson

Judy Garland-The Golden Years at MGM: The Harvey Girls, The Pirate, Summer Stock
Multi Audio ML-104869

(no listing)

A Star Is Born
Columbia Cl-1101
Harmony HS-11366

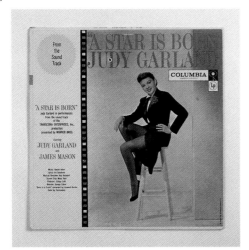

"Gotta Have Me Go With You"
"The Man That Got Away"
"Born in a Trunk"

"Here's What I'm Here For"
"It's a New World"
"Someone at Last"
"Lose That Long Face"

Gay Purr-ee
Warner Bros. B-1479

Overture
"Mewsette" - Robert Goulet
"Little Drops of Rain"
"The Money Cat" - Paul Frees and the Mellow Men
"Portraits of Mewsette" - Instrumental
"Take My Hand Paree"

"Paris Is a Lonely Town"
"Bubbles" - Robert Goulet, Red Buttons, the Mellow Men
"Roses Red, Violets Blue"
"Little Drops of Rain" - Robert Goulet
"Paris Is a Lonely Town" - Instrumental
"The Horse Won't Talk" - Paul Frees
"The Mewsette Finale" (with Robert Goulet and chorus)

Listed chronologically, additional soundtrack recordings include:

Broadway Melody of 1938
Motion Picture Tracks International MPT-3

Babes in Arms
Curtain Calls CC-100/6-6
Sandy Hook SH 2077

Strike Up the Band
Hollywood Soundstage HS-5009
Curtain Calls 100/9-10

Little Nellie Kelly
Cheerio 5000

Girl Crazy
Decca DL-5413
Decca ED-2022
Hollywood Soundstage HS-5008

Thousands Cheer
Hollywood Soundstage 409

Meet Me in St. Louis
Pelican LP-118

The Harvey Girls
Hollywood Soundstage HS-5002

Ziegfeld Follies of 1946
Curtain Calls CC 100/15-16

The Pirate
MGM X-21 (45 rpm)
MGM E-21
MGM E-3234
MGM C-763 (U.K.)
MGM 2-SES-43-ST
MGM 23530

Easter Parade
MGM X-40 (45 rpm)
MGM E-502 (10")
MGM 2-SES-40-ST
MGM E-3227
MGM 23530 (U.K.)
MCA 1459

Words and Music
MGM X-37 (45 rpm)
MGM E-505 (10")
MGM E-3232
MGM E-3771
MGM 53771-ST
MGM Select 2353-033
MCA 25029

In the Good Old Summertime
MGM E-3232
MGM ST-3232
MGM 2-SES-49-ST
MCA 39083

Summer Stock
MGM X-56 (45 rpm)
MGM E-519 (10")
MGM E-3234
MGM 2-SES-52-ST
MCA 39084

Judgment at Nuremberg
MCA 39055
UA UAL-4095

I Could Go On Singing
Capital W-1861
Capital/Belter 20

That's Entertainment
MCA 2-11—2

That's Entertainment, Pt. 2
MGM MG 1-5301

Cut! Out Takes From Hollywood's Greatest Musicals
Out Take Records OF-1,2,3

CDs

Listed alphabetically.

A + E Biography - A Musical Anthology,
Judy Garland
Capital 72434-94750-0-7

American Legends - Judy Garland
Laserlight 12741

Best of Fred Astaire: From MGM Classic Films
MCA MCAD-31175

Best of Gene Kelly: From MGM Classic Films
MCA MCAD-31177

The Best of Judy Garland
MCA HMNCD-015
Eclipse Music Group 64792-2
Intersound Inc. FC-4562
Intersound Inc. CDC-1027
EMI Solo CDSL-8258

Christmas Through the Years - Judy Garland
Laserlight 12534

Decca Presents Judy Garland 1936-1940
MCA 4-11059

Easter Parade
Rhino R2-71960

For Me and My Gal
Rhino R2-72204

Gershwin's Girl Crazy
Rhino R-2-72590

Golden Memories of Judy Garland
Pair PCD-2-1030

Great Ladies of Song: Spotlight on Judy Garland
Capital CDP-7243-8-29396-2-7

The Great MGM Stars - Judy Garland
MGM CDMGM 29

Great Songs from MGM Classic Films
MCA MCAD -31056
MCA MCAD- 31130
MCA MCAD- 31131

Have Yourself a Merry Little Christmas - Lorna Luft, Judy Garland
Carlton Sound 30360-00172

The Hollywood Golden Years, Greatest Original Soundtracks: *Meet Me in St. Louis, The Wizard of Oz, Presenting Lily Mars, Little Nellie Kelly*
Blue Moon MCD-7110

Judy
Capital C.P. 7-92345-2

Judy at Carnegie Hall
Capital C.P.-7-90013-2

Judy at the Palace
MCA MCAD 4-1105

Judy Garland
Rainbow RCD 317
Legends LECD-094

Judy Garland à Paris
Europe 1

Judy Garland - A Star Is Born
Columbia 44389

Judy Garland - A Touch of Class
TC-885302

Judy Garland - America's Treasure
Garland GRZ013

Judy Garland and Bing Crosby - Armed Forces Radio Broadcasts - Mail Call
Laserlight 15413

Judy Garland and Liza Minnelli Together
Curb D2-77587

Judy Garland - Chasing Rainbows
Remember RMB 75007

Judy Garland - Child of Hollywood, Great Original Performances
Robert Parkers Classic Years RPCD 618

The Judy Garland Christmas Album
Laserlight 12467

Judy Garland - Classic Songs From the Stage & Screen
Music Club MCCD-101

Judy Garland - Collection
Columbia VMK-1130

The Judy Garland Collection
Music & Memories MMD1004

Judy Garland - Collector's Gems From the MGM Films
Rhino R-2-772543

Judy Garland - Dear Mr. Gable
MCA MCAD-20540

Judy Garland: From MGM Classic Films
MCA MCAD-31176

Judy Garland Gold Collection
Dejavu 5-130-2

Judy Garland - Golden Greats
MCA MCLD-19045

Judy Garland - Greatest Hits
Curb Records D2-77370

Judy Garland - Her 25 Greatest Hits
The Entertainers CD 0271 AAD

Judy Garland - I'm Always Chasing Rainbows
Pickwick International Inc. (U.K.)

Judy Garland in Concert - the Beginning and the End
Legend CD-6011/6012

Judy Garland in Concert - The Legendary Amsterdam Concert 1960
Intermusic Spain DGB-53044

Judy Garland - *Meet Me in St. Louis*
MCA MCAD 4-11059

Judy Garland on Radio 1936 - 1944
VJC VJC-1043

Judy Garland - Over the Rainbow
CE DE Entertainment CD-66100
Classic Popular CDCD-1137
CMC Home Entertainment 10164-2
Pro Arte CP-547
The Entertainers CD-406-AAD
Avid

The Judy Garland Second Souvenir Album
MCA/Decca MCAD 4-11059

The Judy Garland Show - 50 Hit Songs From the Immortal Judy Garland
Laserlight 15942

The Judy Garland Show - Fly Me to the Moon
Laserlight 12484

Judy Garland Shows on the Air
OTA-101911

Judy Garland - That's Entertainment
Capital CP 7-48426-2
Cema Special Markets CDL-57357

Judy Garland - The Complete Decca Masters
MCA MCAD 4-11059

Judy Garland - The Early Years
Avid Records WEC-319

Judy Garland - *The Harvey Girls*
Rhino R272151

Judy Garland - The Hollywood Years
MCA/Decca MCAD-10504

Judy Garland - The Hollywood Years, vol. 2
MCA/Decca MCAD-10504

Judy Garland - The London Sessions
Capital Masters C.P. 7-99618-2

Judy Garland - The One and Only, vol. 1,2,3,
Capital D-217007

Judy Garland - The Story
Dejavu DVRECD-07

Judy Garland - 25th Anniversary Retrospective
Capital C.P.-7243-29901-2-3

Judy Garland - You Made Me Love You
Carlton Home Entertainment 304592

Judy Garland - *Ziegfeld Girl/For Me and My Gal/ Girl Crazy/Meet Me in St. Louis*
Chansons Cinema

Meet Me in St. Louis
MCA MCAD-11491

Mickey and Judy
Rhino R2-71921

Miss Show Business
Capital C.P. 7-92344-2

My Greatest Songs - Judy Garland
MCD 18351

Over the Rainbow - Judy Garland
MCA MCAD-20214

Over the Rainbow - Judy Garland in Concert
Pickwick PWK-022 (U.K.)

The Pirate
MCA MCAD-5950

A Portrait of Judy Garland
Gallerie GALE 407

Premium Masters - The Great Judy Garland
Castle Communications PCD10186

A Star Is Born
Radiola MR-1155

Summer Stock
MCA MCAD-5948

The Wizard of Oz
Rhino R2-71999
CBS AK-45356

The Wonderful Judy Garland - Zing! Went the Strings of My Heart
Empress RAJCD 873

Words and Music
MCA MCAD-5949

The Young Judy Garland
Pavilion Record PASTCD 7014

The Young Judy Garland - Always Chasing Rainbows
ASV CDAJA-5093

Ziegfeld Follies
MGM Records

Home Video Library

Pigskin Parade
Fox Video 1892

Broadway Melody of 1938
MGM/UA M301048

Thoroughbreds Don't Cry
MGM/UA M202509 B

Everybody Sing
MGM/UA M202506

Listen, Darling
MGM/UA M202508

Love Finds Andy Hardy
MGM/UA M201715

The Wizard of Oz
MGM/UA M600001
MGM/UA M301656

Babes in Arms
MGM/UA M400585

Andy Hardy Meets Debutante
MGM/UA M201720

Strike Up the Band
MGM/UA M400565 B

Little Nellie Kelly
MGM/UA M202507

Ziegfeld Girl/We Must Have Music
MGM/UA M301585

Life Begins for Andy Hardy
MGM/UA M201716

Babes on Broadway
MGM/UA M301677

For Me and My Gal
MGM/UA M201379

Presenting Lily Mars
MGM/UA M300827

Girl Crazy
MGM/UA M300567

Thousands Cheer
MGM/UA M300984

Meet Me in St. Louis
MGM/UA M201827

The Clock
MGM/UA M200890

The Harvey Girls
MGM/UA M301001

Ziegfeld Follies
MGM/UA M600173

Till the Clouds Roll By
MGM/UA M700094

The Pirate
MGM/UA M700101

Easter Parade
MGM/UA M202419

Words and Music
MGM/UA M300861

In the Good Old Summertime
MGM/UA M300860

Summer Stock/Every Sunday
MGM/UA M300851

A Star Is Born
Warner Home Video WHV 11335 A/B

Judgment at Nuremberg
MGM/UA M301536

Gay Purr-ee
Warner Home Video WHV 11500

A Child Is Waiting
MGM/UA M301824

I Could Go On Singing
MGM/UA M301578

That's Entertainment
MGM/UA M600007

That's Entertainment Part II
MGM/UA M70075
MGM/UA M100075

That's Entertainment Part III
MGM/UA M903028

Everybody Sing / Little Nellie Kelly
MGM/UA ML10285

Judy, Judy, Judy
V-Yes 691B

Judy Garland General Electric Theater
MUSIC 60278

The Judy Garland Christmas Show
MGM/UA M602386

Judy Garland in Concert, vol. 1
RKO 3002-B

Judy Garland in Concert, vol. 2
RKO 3003-B

The Judy Garland Show
KOV B-V

Hollywood Musicals of the 50s
Passport Video VS 2225

Table 1: *Wizard of Oz* Collectibles

Product	Manufacturer	Year	Description	Price
Address Book	MGM Grand Hotel, Inc.	1997	cover art illustrated with characters from the film	a.
Banks	Multi Toys	1989	set of four hard plastic banks, 12 inches tall	a.
Bells	The Hamilton Collection	1988	thirteen-piece porcelain series, featuring the film characters & the ruby slippers, 5 inches tall, with a 24k gold band	b. each
Buttons	Economy Novelty & Printing Co.	1939	set of five individually numbered, orange pin-back buttons, 1 1/4 inches in diameter. Issued in Mexico as "El Mago de Oz"	c. each
Buttons	Button-Up Company	1986	set of eight full-color pin-back buttons, featuring MGM characters, with contemporary catch phrases, 1 3/4 inches in diameter, also a set of eight black and white pin-back buttons, featuring actual portraits of the MGM characters, 1 1/2 inches in diameter	a. set
Buttons	Whataburger Restaurants	1989	set of seven full-color pin-back buttons, promoting an Oz drinking glass campaign, featuring MGM characters with contemporary phrases, 3 inches in diameter	b. set
Buttons	unknown	1989	set of four cloisonné buttons, not intended for resale, commemorating Fiftieth Anniversary of the MGM film, 1 1/8-inches in diameter	a. each
Buttons	unknown	1989	"It's Oz Time at Macy's" department store promotional pin-back button, 3 inches in diameter	a.
Calendar	Cleo	1989	"50th Anniversary Commemorative Edition," featuring MGM movie stills and a brief narrative	a.
Christmas Ornaments	Bradford Novelty Company	1977	set of four MGM characters, 4 1/2 inches tall, also boxed set of Christmas balls, featuring scenes from the MGM motion picture	a. each
Christmas Ornaments	Ron Kron	1988	set of five hand-painted MGM characters, limited edition	c. each
Christmas Ornaments	Presents	1989	set of six cloth and vinyl, MGM characters	a. each
Christmas Ornaments	Enesco	1989	set of four hand-painted ornaments made of Artplas, MGM characters, in a limited edition	a. each
Christmas Ornaments	Christopher Radko	1998	glass ornaments featuring the four main characters, plus the ruby slippers. Dorothy and Toto measure 5 inches in height, limited edition	b. each
Christmas Ornaments	The Danbury Mint	1989	set of twelve full-color scenes from the MGM motion picture, framed in a 24k gold border	a. each
Clocks	Westclock	1980s	series of alarm clocks and Oz timepieces, hard plastic and metal	b.
Clocks	Novus Industries	1989	set of two battery-operated wall clocks, made of hard plastic, 10 inches in diameter	a.
Coins	Paramount International Coin Corporation	1989	set of twelve .999 silver proofs, with a custom display case featuring MGM characters, 38.40 mm in diameter	g. set
Coins	Paramount International Coin Corporation	1989	set of six .999 gold proofs, limited edition ten thousand pieces, 20mm in diameter	i. set
Coloring Book	Hutchinson Publishing	1940	cover art features MGM characters based on W.W. Denslow's original artwork	e.
Coloring Book	Parkes Run Publishing	1972	"Giant Story Coloring Book" cover art features 1972 theatrical re-release poster from the MGM motion picture, 17 inches x 22 inches	b.
Coloring Book	Aero Educational Products	1977	"Judy Garland as Dorothy in The Wizard of Oz Coloring Book," featuring drawings based on the MGM motion picture	a.
Coloring Book	Golden Books	1988	"Big Color Activity Book," featuring drawings from the MGM motion picture	a.
Comic Books	Marvel and DC Comics	1975	"MGM's Marvelous Wizard of Oz," character drawings based on the MGM motion picture	b.
Cookie Jar	Clay Art	1990	white ceramic jar, featuring relief figures of the four main MGM characters	c.
Cookie Jar	The Warner Bros. Studio Store	1998	white ceramic jar, featuring relief figures of Dorothy and the Wicked Witch, jar is shaped as the Kansas farmhouse	b.
Crayon Box	Cheinco Plaything's	1975	metal container featuring the four main MGM characters, holds over 100 crayons	a.
Cups & Glasses	Corning Glass Works	1939	set of eight tumblers, illustrated with MGM characters, issued weekly by Sealtest Cottage Cheese	b. each
Cups & Glasses	Mann Theaters	1974	theater chain promotional give-away, with purchase of a large soft drink, featuring the four main MGM characters	a.
Cups & Glasses	Dunkin' Donuts	1975	set of promotional tumblers	a.
Cups & Glasses	unknown	1980s	ceramic mug, illustrated with the MGM characters and the Haunted Forest	a.
Cups & Glasses	Kentucky Fried Chicken	1984	set of four fast-food chain premium glasses, featuring MGM characters	a.
Cups & Glasses	Whataburger Restaurants	1989	commemorative of the Fiftieth Anniversary of the MGM motion picture, a Coca-Cola premium with purchase	a.
Cups & Glasses	Krystal Restaurants	1989	set of six glasses, a weekly Coca-Cola premium with purchase	a.
Cups & Glasses	Whirley Industries, Inc.	1989	plastic mug, "The Wizard of Oz Live!" a national stage show tour	a.
Cups & Glasses	Paper Art Company	1989	hot and cold paper cups, plates, party accessories	a.
Cups & Glasses	The Hamilton Collection	1990	set of ceramic mugs, illustrated with the MGM characters	a.
Cups & Glasses	Sterling Products, Inc.	1990	plastic drinking cup, illustrated with the MGM characters	a.

Item	Manufacturer	Year	Description	
Découpage Kit	Friends Industries	1975	boxed set, containing two wooden plaques and materials	a.
Dorothy Costume	Ben Cooper	1975	plastic face mask, with a vinyl Halloween costume	b.
Dorothy Costume	Collegeville	1989	plastic face mask with vinyl body suit, deluxe costume made of cotton, sizes for adults and children	b.
Dorothy Costume	The Warner Bros. Studio Store	1998	blue and white cotton gingham, kids sizes: s, m, l	b.
Dorothy Doll	Lastic Plastic Company	1961	vinyl head and arms on a cloth body, rooted synthetic hair	f.
Dorothy Doll	Mego Toys Corporation	1974	vinyl head on a stuffed cloth body, synthetic rooted hair, 14 inches tall	b.
Dorothy Doll	Marjore Spangler	1979	vinyl doll, rooted synthetic hair, fully jointed, 15 inches tall, limited edition	d.
Dorothy Doll	Dave Grossman Designs	1982	porcelain with glass eyes, hand-painted, limited edition of 250, 15 inches tall, mounted to interconnecting Yellow Brick Road stand	h.
Dorothy Doll	Ideal	1984	vinyl doll, 9 inches tall, with Toto	b.
Dorothy Doll	Effanbee	1985	vinyl doll, rooted synthetic hair, 11 1/2 inches tall	b.
Dorothy Doll	Largo Toys	1989	cloth rag doll	b.
Dorothy Doll	Applause, Inc.	1989	cloth rag doll, sold as a souvenir of the stage production "The Wizard of Oz Live!"	b.
Dorothy Doll	Warner Bros. Studio Store	1998	15-inch soft vinyl and cloth doll from the Yellow Brick Road Collection. 1st in the series "Judy Garland as Dorothy." Gift boxed with hard plastic basket and dog, Toto.	a.
Erasers	Applause	1989	six MGM characters	a. set
Figurines	Seymour Mann	1974	hand-painted, porcelain	b.
Figurines	Seymour Mann	1981-83	hand-painted, porcelain, 6 1/2 inches tall	b.
Figurines	Goebel	1980s	hand-painted, fine porcelain, created by Kramlik Porcelain Studio, limited edition	g.
Figurines	Avon	1985	"Images of Hollywood" collection, porcelain, 5 1/2 inches tall	b.
Figurines	The Franklin Mint	1988	"The Wizard of Oz Portrait Sculpture Collection," featuring twenty hand-painted, porcelain figurines, Emerald City display case	b. each
Figurines	Presents	1988	hard plastic, 3 3/4 inches tall	a.
Figurines	Multi Toys	1989	set of six poseable figures, sold separately or in sets, 4 inches tall	a. each
Figurines	Just Toys	1989	bendable figures	a.
Figurines	Dave Grossman Creations		cast marble, limited edition	c.
Figurines	The Metropolitan Guild for Collectible Art	1989	sculpted by artist Carver E. Tripp, finished in 24k gold, 4 inches tall	a.
Figurines	The Franklin Mint	1991	"Judy Garland as Dorothy," hand-painted, bisque porcelain, 8 1/2 inches tall	c.
Flag	The Warner Bros. Studio Store	1998	made of nylon measuring 28 inches x 43 inches, pictured are the ruby slippers and the Yellow Brick Road	a.
Games	Whitman	1939	movie tie-in board game	e.
Games	Castell Brothers Ltd.	1940	card game, illustrated with hand-tinted color MGM motion picture stills, British	f.
Games	Parker Bros.	1998	Monopoly ™, Wizard of Oz edition	b.
Gumball Machine	The Warner Bros. Studio Store	1998	features Dorothy and Glinda figurines on top	b.
Lunch Kit	Aladden Industries	1989	plastic lunch pail and thermos	a.
Magnets	Grynnen Barrett	1987	six character boxed set	a.
Magnets	Vanderbilt Products	1989	various MGM characters and scenes	a.
Music Boxes	Schmid	1983	set of four porcelain figural boxes, MGM characters, Judy Garland as Dorothy, plays "Over the Rainbow"	b. each
Music Boxes	Presents	1988	set of seven jewelry boxes, featuring MGM scenes featuring songs from the motion picture	b. each
Music Boxes	Enesco	1988	set of six Jack-in-the-boxes, available in two sizes, smaller version is animated, limited edition	d. each
Music Boxes	Enesco	1989	set of five revolving figurines, Dorothy figure plays "Over the Rainbow," "The Yellow Brick Road," musical features the four main characters	b. each
Music Boxes	Presents	1989	set of six revolving figurines, hard-plastic, Dorothy figure plays "Over the Rainbow"	a. each
Music Boxes	The Franklin Mint	1989	series of glass dome musicals, hand-painted, sculpted porcelain, 6 1/2 inches tall	e. each
Night Shirt	The Warner Bros. Studio Store	1998	pictured are the ruby slippers with the caption "It's the shoes," one size fits all	a.
Paint Sets	Friends Industries	1975	"Cast 'N Paint" set includes six plaster figures and materials	a.
Paint Sets	Craft House	1979	"Fast Dry Acrylic Paint By Number"	a.
Paint Sets	Art Award	1989	set of four craft kits, paint-by-number and paint with crayons	a. each
Picture Books	Bobbs-Merrill	1939	L. Frank Baum's book, illustrated with MGM motion picture stills	c.
Picture Books	Hutchinson Publishing	1940	"photoplay" edition of the L.Frank Baum novel, featuring "coloured" dust jacket, illustrated with eight movie stills, British	g.
Picture Books	Hutchinson Publishing	1940	paperback of the Baum novel with MGM cover art, featuring original W.W. Denslow drawings, British	d.
Picture Books	MGM Merchandising	1970	"special edition" in association with the Singer Sewing Machine Co., and the 1970 television broadcast, illustrated with MGM scenes	b.
Picture Books	Grossett & Dunlap	1976	"movie edition" illustrated with MGM scenes	a.
Picture Books	Harper & Row	1976	"movie edition" illustrated with MGM scenes	a.
Picture Books	Ottenheimer	1977	"See-Thru Picture Storybook"	a.
Picture Books	Doubleday	1978	illustrated with twenty-four MGM scenes, introduction by Ray Bolger	a.
Picture Books	Western Publishing	1989	"The Wizard of Oz, Movie Storybook," illustrated with MGM scenes	a.
Pillbox	The Warner Bros. Studio Store	1997	gold finish with red rhinestones forming Judy Garland's ruby slippers	b.

Pillow	Modern Pillow Co.	1970s	color artwork, adapted from the 1972 theatrical re-issue poster	b.
Pillow Case	Associated Marketing	1989	featuring the four main MGM characters, fits standard size pillow	a.
Placemats	Dow Brands	1989	set of two with proof of purchase from ZIPLOCK Brand Storage Bags, Handi-Wrap, or Saran Wrap, depicting MGM characters	a.
Plates	Knowles China Company	1977-79	set of eight porcelain collectors plates, illustrated by artist James A. Auckland, first in the series, "Over the Rainbow," limited edition	b. each
Plates	The Hamilton Collection	1988	set of eight porcelain collectors plates illustrated by artist Thomas Blackshear, limited edition, featuring a 23K gold "Yellow Brick Road" rim	b. each
Plates	The Hamilton Collection	1990	"Fifty Years of Oz" porcelain collectors plate, by artist Thomas Blackshear, limited edition	b.
Porcelain Box	The Warner Bros. Studio Store	1998	Dorothy figurine on a porcelain box measuring 3 1/4 inches tall, inside box reads "There's no place like home," first in the series.	a.
Puppet	Multi Toys Corp.	1989	set of six, vinyl and cloth hand-puppets	a.
Puzzle	Jaymar	1960s	set of five 17 inches x 22 inches, 100 pieces	a. each
Puzzles	Doug Smith Productions	1977	set of four frame-tray puzzles, 17 inches x 22 inch	a. each
Puzzles	Effanbee	1984	"Legend Doll Series," canister packaging with a 12-piece puzzle	a.
Puzzles	Western Publishing Co.	1989	series of frame-tray and boxed jigsaw puzzles, 100 pieces	a.
Puzzles	Milton Bradley	1990	"Classic Movie Puzzle" series, features artwork from the 1989 Norman James Company movie poster, 1000 pieces	a.
Puzzles	Puzzling Pieces	1990s	series featuring MGM scenes, 24 pieces	a.
Puzzles	The Warner Bros. Studio Store	1998	set of two puzzles featuring MGM scenes, 1000 pieces	a.
Rubber Stamps	Multi Toys	1989	set of twelve figural inking stamps	a.
Rubber Stamps	All Night Media	1989	set of eleven wood-mounted rubber inking stamps	a.
Rubber Stamps	All Night Media	1989	set of eighteen inking stamps	a. each, b. set
Ruby Slippers	The Warner Bros. Studio Store	1997	children's red glitter slippers, sizes 8 - 13, 1-2	a.
Ruler	MGM Grand Hotel, Inc.	1997	12 inches plastic, featuring colorful drawings of the MGM characters	a.
Salt and Pepper Shakers	The Warner Bros. Studio Store	1998	series of four, 4 1/2 inches tall	a.
Scarf	Wendy Gell Jewelry	1989	cotton, depicting MGM characters on a background of poppies	b.
Sheets	Perfect Fit Industries	1976	poly-cotton, no-iron sheets and pillow cases, MGM characters	b.
Snow Globe	The Warner Bros. Studio Store	1998	glass dome, 8 inches tall, featuring Dorothy, Glinda in a bubble	b.
Song Book	Publishing International	1996	"Play-a-Long" keyboard, featuring songs from the MGM motion picture, illustrated with MGM stills, batteries included	a.
Stand-Up Figures	Triangle Enterprises	1990	cardboard "Stand-Me-Up" figures	a.
Stationary	Whitman	1939	"The Wizard of Oz Children's Writing Paper," featuring Al Hirschfeld illustrations, 10 sheets with envelopes, boxed	e.
Stationary	Applause	1998	set of four note pads	a.
Stickers	Multi Toys	1989	vinyl stickers, MGM characters	a.
Stickers	Western Publishing	1998	"Sticker Fun," containing twenty pre-cut stickers, MGM characters	a.
Straws	Multi Toys	1989	set of twelve "Snack 'N Sip Pals" drinking straws, featuring MGM characters	a.
Suncatchers	Vanderbilt Products, Inc.	1989	series of hanging, stained-glass/plastic window ornaments	a.
Sunglasses	Multi Toys	1989	"Fun Shades," available in six colors	a.
Tins	Cheinco Plaything's	1975	crayon box, illustrated with MGM characters a.	
Tins	Presents	1988	set of five, sold with or without miniature Oz playing cards	a. each
Tins	Holiday Delites	1989	six-ounce, twelve-ounce, and two-pound containers, filled with candies, butter cookies, popcorn	a. each
Towel	The Franco Company	1977	calendar beach towel, printed in Romania, featuring MGM characters	a.
Towel	Renaissance	1988	Beach towel 30 inch x 60 inch, MGM characters	b.
Trash Can	Cheinco USA	1975	metal can, colorful artwork of the MGM Characters	a.
Wristwatch	unknown	1989	vinyl and plastic, souvenir of "The Wizard of Oz Live!"	a.
Wristwatch	Macy's	1989	"It's Oz Time at Macy's," 50th anniversary department store commemorative.	b.
Wristwatch	E.K.O.	1989	child-size quartz wristwatch	b.

Sources

Autographs

Thomas Platt
66 Witherspoon St.
Princeton, NJ 08542
609-921-0856

Cockamamie's
Herb Millman & John Dwyer
9A West Bridge Street
New Hope, PA 18938
215-862-5454
http://www.newhopeonline.com

Books/Oz & Related

Books of Wonder
16 West 18th Street
New York, NY 10011
212-989-3270

Clubs

The International Judy Garland Club
Membership Correspondence to:
Roger Cogar
252 Tithepit Shaw Lane
Warlington, England CR6 9AQ

The International Wizard of Oz Club, Inc.
Membership Correspondence to:
Fred M. Myer, Secretary
220 North 11th Street
Escanaba, MI 49829
Dues: $10.00

Collectibles

The 5 & Dime
40 North Union Street
Lambertville, NJ 07087
609-397-4957

Hake's Americana & Collectibles
P. O. Box 1444
York, PA 17405
Mail Order Auction Catalog $5.00

John C. Van Doren
60 Wagner Road
Stockton, NJ 08559
1-888-397-4803 (toll free)
S.A.S.E. for Mail Order Catalog details. Specializing in
vintage paper items; magazines, sheet music, posters
& lobby cards, paper dolls, coloring books, original stills.

Dolls

Collector's United
711 South 3rd Avenue
Chatsworth, GA 30705
706-695-8242
Monthly publication, dolls & related classifieds. Buy-Sell-Trade.
One-year subscription: $36.00

Movie Posters & Lobby Cards

Movie Art
Kirby McDaniel
P. O. Box 164291
Austin, TX 78716
512-479-6680

Collecting Hollywood
P. O. Box 2512
Chattanooga, TN 37409
1-800-673-0460
Monthly publication, dealer classifieds.
One-year subscription: $40.00

Photography

Philip Isaiah Katz
Blackfan Studio
P. O. Box 368
New Hope, PA 18938
215-862-3503
215-862-3902 fax
Email: PIKFan@aol.com
http://www.Blackfanstudio.com

Records

The Record Collector
1 Bridge Street
Morrisville, PA 19067
215-295-5199
Soundtracks & Personalities 33 1/3 rpm

Stills

Cinema Collectors
1507 Wilcox Avenue
Hollywood, CA 90028
213-461-6516

Jerry Ohlinger's Movie Material
242 West 14th Street
New York, NY 10011
212-989-0869

Movie Star News
134 West 18th Street
New York, NY 10011
212-620-8160

Bibliography

To learn more about the life and career of Judy Garland, the author recommends the following books:

Finch, Christopher. *Rainbow, The Stormy Life of Judy Garland*. New York: Grosset & Dunlap, 1975.

Frank, Gerold. *Judy*. New York: Harper & Row, 1975.

Fricke, John. *Judy Garland, World's Greatest Entertainer*. New York: Henry Holt, 1992.

Fricke, John. *The Wizard of Oz, The Official 50th Anniversary Pictorial History*. New York: Warner Books, 1989.

Minnelli, Vincente, with Arce, Hector. *I Remember It Well*. New York: Doubleday, 1974.

Other Garland biographies and sources of information include:

Barson, Michael S. *Judy, Liza, The Myth and the Madness*. New York: Cresskill, Sharon Publications, 1985.

Cox, Stephen. *The Munchkins Remember, The Wizard of Oz and Beyond*. New York: E.P. Dutton, 1989.

Dahl, David, and Kehne, Barry. *Young Judy*. New York: Mason/Charter, 1975.

Deans, Mickey, and Pinchot, Ann. *Weep No More, My Lady*. New York: Hawthorn, 1972.

DiOrio, Al. *Little Girl Lost, The Life and Hard Times of Judy Garland*. London: Coronet, 1973.

Edwards, Anne. *Judy Garland*. New York: Simon and Schuster, 1975.

Harmetz, Aljean. *The Making of The Wizard of Oz*. New York: Limelight Editions, 1984.

Harnne, Howard. *The Judy Garland Souvenir Songbook*. New York: Chappell Music, 1975.

Haver, Ronald. *A Star Is Born*. New York: Alfred A. Knopf, 1988.

Juneau, James. *Judy Garland*. New York: Pyramid Publications, 1975.

Luft, Lorna. *Me and My Shadows*. New York: Pocket Books, 1998.

McClelland, Doug. *Down The Yellow Brick Road: The Making of The Wizard of Oz*. New York: Pyramid Publications, 1976.

Melton, David. *Judy: A Remembrance*. Hollywood: Stanyan Books, 1972.

Morella, Joe, and Epstein, Edward. *Judy. The Films and Career of Judy Garland*. New York: Cadillac Publishing/Citadel Press, 1969.

Parish, James Robert, and Bowers, Ronald L. *The Golden Era, the MGM Stock Company*. New York: Arlington House, 1973.

Rust, Brian. *The Complete Entertainment Discography, 1890s-1942*. New York: Arlington House, 1973.

Sanders, Coyne Steven. *Rainbows End*. New York: William Marrow and Company, Inc., 1990.

Shipman, David. *Judy Garland, The Secret Life of An American Legend*. New York: Hyperion, 1993.

Smith, Lorna. *Judy With Love*. London: Robert Hale & Company, 1975.

Spada, James. *Judy & Liza*. Garden City, New York: Dolphin/Doubleday & Company, Inc., 1983.

Stubblebine, Donald J. *Cinema Sheet Music, A Comprehensive Listing of Published Film Music from Squaw Man (1914) to Batman (1989)*. Jefferson, North Carolina: McFarland & Company, 1991.

Thomas, Rhys. *The Ruby Slippers of Oz*. Los Angeles: Tale Weaver Publishing, 1989.

Vare, Ethlie Ann. *Rainbow, A Star-Studded Tribute to Judy Garland*. New York: Boulevard Books, 1998.

Watson, Thomas J., and Chapman, Bill. *Judy: Portrait of An American Legend*. New York: McGraw Hill, 1986.

Magazine covers are from the following sources:

American Classic Screen, published by The Traditions Press, cover art by John Tibbetts.

Film Careers, published by Clare House, cover photographs from the Columbia Broadcasting System.

Film Review, published by ABC Chatter.

Hollywood Studio Magazine, published by Hollywood Studio Magazine, Inc.

Hollywood Who's Who, published by Dell Publishing Company, Inc.

Judy Garland, A Special Tribute Issue, published by Skywald Publishing Corporation, cover art painting by Brendan Lynch.

Look, published by Look, Inc., and by Cowles Magazines, Inc., 1/2/40 cover photographed by Willinger, 5/7/40 cover photographed by Eric Carpenter, 10/8/40 cover photographed by Earl Theisen, 3/22/55 cover photographed by Milton H. Greene, 4/10/62 cover photographed by Douglas Kirkland.

Modern Screen, published by the Dell Publishing Company, Inc.

Movieland, published by Movieland, Inc., 12/43 cover photographed by Tom Kelley.

Movie Life, published by Ideal Publishing Corp., 12/44 cover photographed by Eric Carpenter, chief staff photographer Arnold Johnson, and photo manager and photographer Mel Traxel.

Movie Mirror, published by MacFadden Publications, Inc., 8/40 cover photographed by Paul Duval.

Movie Portraits, published by Ideal Publishing Corp.

Movie-Radio Guide, published by Triangle Publications, Inc., 10/5/40 cover photographed by Eddie Cronenweth, 4/19/41 cover photographed by Jack Albin, 9/13/41 cover photographed by Bruce Bailey.

Movie Show, published by Liberty Magazine, Inc., staff photographer Jack Albin.

Movie Stars Parade, published by Ideal Publishing Corp., 12/45 cover photographed by Eric Carpenter, staff photographer Mel Traxel, and assistant photographers Leroy Zeigler & Arnold Johnson.

Movie Story Magazine, published by Fawcett Publications, Inc.

Parade, published by Parade Publications, The Columbus Citizen, published by Scripps-Howard.

Photoplay, published by Macfadden Publications, Inc., 12/40 cover photographed by Paul Hesse.

Photoplay/Movie Mirror, published by Macfadden Publications, Inc., 8/41 cover photographed by Willinger, 7/42, 7/43, & 11/44 covers photographed by Paul Hesse.

Picture Show, published by The Amalgamated Press, Ltd.

Redbook, published by McCall Corporation, cover photograph by Pat Clark-Warner Brothers.

Screen Guide, published by Triangle Publications, Inc., 3/41 cover photographed by Jack Albin, 11/45 cover photographed by Bruce Bailey.

Screen and Television Guide, published by Hillman Periodicals, Inc., staff photographers Walt Davis & Joe Shere.

Screen Album, published by Dell Publishing Company, Inc.

Screenland, published by Screenland Magazine, Inc., 7/40 art director Frank J. Carroll.

Screenland, published by Hunter Publications, Inc., staff photographer Jean Duval.

Screenland, published by Liberty Magazine, Inc., 3/46 cover photographed by Eric Carpenter.

Screen Life, published by Skye Publication Company, Inc., staff photographers G.K. Livitsanos, Frank Worth, & Robert Perkins, 1/55 cover photograph from Warner Bros. "A Star Is Born."

Screen Romances, published by the Dell Publishing Company, Inc., staff photographer Walt Davis.

Screen Stories, published by the Dell Publishing Company, Inc., staff photographers Bob Beerman & Bert Parry.

Show, published by Hartford Publications, Inc., art director Henry Wolf.

Silver Screen, published by Liberty Magazine, Inc., staff photographer Jack Albin.

Woman's Day, published by Sungravure Pty. Ltd.

Photo Credits

Original poster art, lobby cards, and ad art from the following motion pictures appear courtesy of Warner Bros. Worldwide Publishing/Turner Entertainment: *Andy Hardy Meets Debutante* ©1940 Loew's Incorporated. Renewed © 1967 Metro-Goldwyn-Mayer, Inc. All rights reserved; *Babes in Arms* © 1939 Loew's Incorporated. Renewed © 1966 Metro-Goldwyn-Mayer, Inc. All rights reserved; *Babes on Broadway* © 1941 Loew's Incorporated. Renewed © 1968 Metro-Goldwyn-Mayer, Inc. All rights reserved; *Broadway Melody of 1938* © 1937 Metro-Goldwyn-Mayer Corporation. Renewed © 1964 Metro-Goldwyn-Mayer, Inc. All rights reserved; *The Clock* © 1945 Loew's Incorporated. Renewed © 1972 Metro-Goldwyn-Mayer, Inc. All rights reserved; *Easter Parade* © 1948 Loew's Incorporated. Renewed © 1975 Metro-Goldwyn-Mayer, Inc. All rights reserved; *Every Sunday* © 1936 Metro-Goldwyn-Mayer Corporation. Renewed © 1963 Metro-Goldwyn-Mayer, Inc. All rights reserved; *Everybody Sing* © 1938 Loew's Incorporated. Renewed © 1965 Metro-Goldwyn-Mayer, Inc. All rights reserved; *For Me and My Gal* © 1942 Loew's Incorporated. Renewed © 1969 Metro-Goldwyn-Mayer, Inc. All rights reserved; *Girl Crazy* © 1943 Loew's Incorporated. Renewed © 1970 Metro-Goldwyn-Mayer, Inc. All rights reserved; *The Harvey Girls* © 1945 Loew's Incorporated. Renewed © 1973 Metro-Goldwyn-Mayer, Inc. All rights reserved; *In the Good Old Summertime* © 1949 Loew's Incorporated. Renewed © 1976 Metro-Goldwyn-Mayer, Inc. All rights reserved; *Life Begins for Andy Hardy* © 1941 Loew's Incorporated. Renewed © 1968 Metro-Goldwyn-Mayer, Inc. All rights reserved; *Listen, Darling* © 1938 Loew's Incorporated. Renewed © 1965 Metro-Goldwyn-Mayer, Inc. All rights reserved; *Little Nellie Kelly* © 1940 Loew's Incorporated. Renewed © 1967 Metro-Goldwyn-Mayer, Inc. All rights reserved; *Love Finds Andy Hardy* © 1938 Loew's Incorporated. Renewed © 1965 Metro-Goldwyn-Mayer, Inc. All rights reserved; *Meet Me in St. Louis* © 1944 Loew's Incorporated. Renewed © 1971 Metro-Goldwyn-Mayer, Inc. All rights reserved; *The Pirate* © 1948 Loew's Incorporated. Renewed © 1975 Metro-Goldwyn-Mayer, Inc. All rights reserved; *Presenting Lily Mars* © 1943 Loew's Incorporated. Renewed © 1970 Metro-Goldwyn-Mayer, Inc. All rights reserved; *Strike Up the Band* © 1940 Loew's Incorporated. Renewed © 1967 Metro-Goldwyn-Mayer, Inc. All rights reserved; *Summer Stock* © 1950 Loew's Incorporated. Renewed © 1977 Metro-Goldwyn-Mayer, Inc. All rights reserved; *Thoroughbreds Don't Cry* © 1937 Metro-Goldwyn-Mayer Corporation. Renewed © 1964 Metro-Goldwyn-Mayer, Inc. All rights reserved; *Thousands Cheer* © 1943 Loew's Incorporated. Renewed © 1970 Metro-Goldwyn-Mayer, Inc. All rights reserved; *Till the Clouds Roll By* © 1946 Loew's Incorporated. Renewed © 1973 Metro-Goldwyn-Mayer, Inc. All rights reserved; *The Wizard of Oz* © 1939 Loew's Incorporated. Renewed © 1966 Metro-Goldwyn-Mayer, Inc. All rights reserved; *Words and Music* © 1948 Loew's Incorporated. Renewed © 1975. All rights reserved; *Ziegfeld Follies* © 1946 Loew's Incorporated. Renewed © 1973 Metro-Goldwyn-Mayer, Inc. All rights reserved; *Ziegfeld Girl* © 1941 Loew's Incorporated. Renewed © 1968 Metro-Goldwyn-Mayer, Inc. All rights reserved.

Stills from *Pigskin Parade* ©1937 Twentieth Century Fox Film Corporation. Renewed © 1964 Twentieth Century Fox Film Corporation. All rights reserved.

Posters and lobby cards from *A Star Is Born* ©1954 Warner Bros. All rights reserved; *Gay Purr-ee* © 1962. Warner Bros. All rights reserved; *Judgment at Nuremberg* ©1964 RoxLom Films, Inc. All rights reserved; *A Child Is Waiting* ©1962 Larcas Productions, Inc. All rights reserved; *I Could Go On Singing* ©1963 Millar-Turman Productions, Inc. All rights reserved.

All of the illustration material gathered in this book comes from the author's private collection and through the generosity of the following sources.

Woolsey Ackerman: pages 6C; 21B, TR; 22C, BL, BR; 24CL; 25-39; 41-44; 45TL, TR; 46; 50; 51; 53CL; 54C, TR; 55CL, CB, CR; 57BR; 58TL, TR; 60L; 69TR; 74T, BC; 77TL, BL; 87; 90TL, TR, BL, BR; 92TL; 93TL; 96L, BR; 98BL, BC, BR; 100TL; 101TL; 102TR; 103BL, BR; 106; 107TL, TR; 108TL, BR; 111B; 115; 116B; 117; 118.

Michael Siewert: pages 14L; 22BC; 23TR; 44BL, BR, CR; 45CL, C, CR, BL, BC, BR; 47; 48TL, TC, TR; 49; 52T; 53CR; 54TL, CR; 55TL, TC, TR; 56CL; 57TC, TR, CL, CR; 58BL; 59TR, BR; 60TR, CR, BR; 61TL, CL, BL, BC; 62TL, TR, BR; 63TL, TR, BL; 64BL; 65-67; 69BR; 70TL; 71BR; 72TL; 73BR; 74T; 76BR; 78TL, BC; 79TR, BL, BC, BR; 80TR, BR; 81TL, TR; 82T, BL, C, R; 83TL, TC, BL, BR; 84-86; 91TC; 92TL; 94TL, BL; 95R; 96TR; 97TL, BL, BR; 99TL, TR, BL; 100C, BL; 101TR, CR, BL, BR; 102BL, BR; 104; 105T, CL, CR; 106TL; 107CL, BR; 108TR, BL; 109; 116C; 118; 127TL; 128TL, TR; 129TL; 130TR; 138C; 139; 143TR; 144-146.

John C. Van Doren: pages 57TL; 62BL; 68BL; 69TL; 70TR, BR; 71TC; 72BR; 74TR; 75TR; 76TL; 77TR, BR; 78TC; 79TL, BR; 80BL; 81TL, BL, BR; 83TR.

Marge Meisinger: pages 22C; 23TL; 24TL; 52CR, BR; 53TR; 54TC, BR; 88TL; 90C; 94TR; 97TR; 98TL; 100BR; 102TL.

Fred McFadden: pages 64CR, 70BL, 73BL, 78BR, 91TL.

Herb Millman: page 24CR.

Jim and Merlyn Collings: page 88B.

The Academy of Motion Picture Arts & Sciences, Margaret Herrick Library: pages 5, 7TR, 11, 13R.

TOP: T	TOP RIGHT: TR
CENTER: C	CENTER LEFT: CL
BOTTOM: B	CENTER RIGHT: CR
LEFT: L	BOTTOM LEFT: BL
RIGHT: R	BOTTOM CENTER: BC
TOP LEFT: TL	BOTTOM RIGHT: BR
TOP CENTER: TC	

Covers of Gold: Collectible Sheet Music Sports, Fashion, Illustration, & the Dance
Marion Short. Covers of Gold is the third ground-breaking book about collectible sheet music by Marion Short. Exciting new categories covered in this book include baseball music, the evolution of fashion, the Big Band era, and the elusive sheet music cover illustrators. These subjects and more are accompanied by over 550 full color photographs of the actual music, encompassing the approximate time span of 1900 to 1940. Covers of Gold follows the success of Marion Short's first two books, The Gold in Your Piano Bench and More Gold in Your Piano Bench also available from Schiffer Publishing.

Size: 8 1/2" x 11"	591 color photos	160 pp.
Price Guide		Index
ISBN: 0-7643-0105-5	soft cover	$29.95

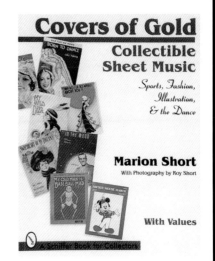

Collectible Sheet Music: From Footlights to "The Flickers": Broadway Shows and Silent Movies Marion Short. From Footlights to "The Flickers" is the long awaited fourth book in the collectible sheet music series by Marion Short. Two of the most popular collecting categories are covered in this colorful book—the music of the Broadway stage, and silent screen movie music. Over 560 full color photographs of sheet music covers from musical shows and silent movies accompany the informative text. The movie songs are arranged alphabetically by cover personality, and the section becomes a compendium of all the major silent screen stars from the earliest days of the "flickers" to the sound revolution in 1929. From Footlights to "The Flickers" follows the success of Mrs. Short's other books about sheet music, The Gold in Your Piano Bench (tearjerkers, black songs, rags, and blues), More Gold in Your Piano Bench (inventions, wars, and disasters), and Covers of Gold (sports, fashion, illustration, and the dance).

Size: 8 1/2" x 11"	561 color photos	188 pp.
Price Guide		
ISBN:0-7643-0552-2	soft cover	$29.95

Hollywood Movie Songs: Collectible Sheet Music Marion Short. *Hollywood Movie Songs* is the fifth book in Marion Short's popular series about collectible sheet music, taking up where she left off in *From Footlights to "The Flickers."* This time she concentrates on movie music after sound took over. The golden years, from dazzling Busby Berkeley movies of the 1930s to the present day, are presented in an exciting kaleidoscope of more than 700 colorful and dramatic sheet music covers from famous movies that feature photos of the world's most beloved film stars. The first section sets the stage for the new Hollywood that took on the challenge of adding sound to motion pictures. The second part features brief biographical sketches of 170 well-known film stars with a listing of their movies that yielded sheet music, and representative photos of each star on selected movie covers. This book also includes extensive indexes of songs, stars, and movies, and a thoughtful price guide that will prove invaluable to movie buffs, nostalgia seekers, and dedicated sheet music collectors.

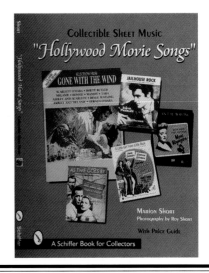

Size: 8 1/2" x 11"	704 color photos	160 pp.
Price Guide		
ISBN: 0-7643-0698-7	soft cover	$29.95

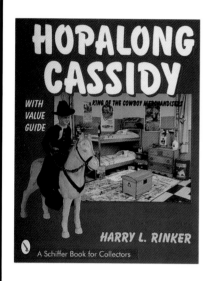

Hopalong Cassidy: King Of The Cowboy Merchandiser Harry L. Rinker. This comprehensive book by one America's foremost authorities on antiques in general, and Hoppy in particular, will introduce you to the various collecting categories within the wonderful world of Hoppy collectibles and allow you to cast your cares aside while leisurely strolling down nostalgia lane. Packed with useful information, it also has beautiful color photographs of most of the merchandise bearing the Hopalong Cassidy name. If you are old enough to have grown up with Hoppy, you will think "I owned one of those" or "I remember one of those." If you are not, you will be moved to say — "Wow! That's neat. I won't mind owning one."

Size: 8 1/2" x 11"   340 color photos   160 pp.
Price Guide
ISBN: 0-87740-765-X   soft cover $29.95

The Queens of Burlesque: Vintage Photographs from the 1940s and 1950s
Len Rothe. For the first time, stunning images of the women of the burlesque stage are gathered together in one great volume. In period photographs the timeless beauty of those exotic women who titillated, teased, and sometimes tortured their audiences is captured and celebrated. These memorable images make it clear that, when it comes to a beautiful body and a gorgeous face, tastes change very little. And just as in the past, the imagination is encouraged to run wild and ponder what might have been. This is a book to relax with and enjoy over and over again. Its rich, nostalgic view of a bygone era in American entertainment will please everyone, men and women alike. A "revealing" piece of Americana!

Size: 8 1/2" x 11"   106 Black & White photos   112 pp.
ISBN: 0-7643-0449-6   soft cover $19.95

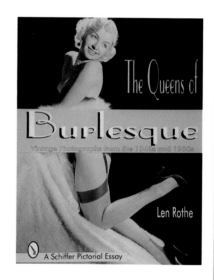

The Bare Truth: The Stars of Burlesque Len Rothe. Following the tremendous success of his first book on the subject, *The Queens of Burlesque*, Len Rothe has again pulled from his collection of original photographs of entertainers this delightful selection of over 100 images of Burlesque stars. Together with a revealing text that introduces burlesque to today's new audience, these photographs retain the surprise and teasing elements that endeared the dancers on stage in the heydays of burlesque shows, before television. In theaters throughout America, striptease dancers entertained grateful audiences. Here are Tempest Storm, Scarlett O'Hara, Lili St. Cyr, Georgia Sothern, and Zorita and her doves. With this book, they look out again with timeless beauty and show you the Bare Truth.

Size: 81/2" x 11"   100 Black & White photos   112 pp.
ISBN: 0-7643-0603-0   soft cover $19.95

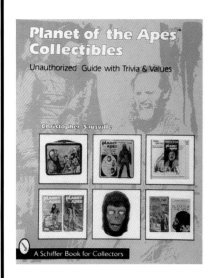

Planet of the Apes Collectibles: An Unauthorized Guide with Trivia & Values Christopher Sausville. Collectors, science fiction fans, and movie aficionados will all go ape over this thorough and entertaining guide to the Planet of the Apes. A detailed listing of collectibles from the original film, the sequels, the television series, and the animated cartoon are all presented. Over 330 color photographs accompany the text. Values are provided for every item listed in the collector's guide. The author also provides a test of every fan's memory with his trivia challenge. Black and white stills from the original movie are found throughout the quiz, adding to the enjoyment and, with a little luck, jogging the memories of all who see them. Finally, a bibliography of Apes references rounds out the presentation.

Size: 8 1/2" x 11"	330 color photos	129 pp.
Price Guide		Index
ISBN: 0-7643-0332-5	soft cover	$29.95

Guide to Tarzan Collectibles Glenn Erardi. One of the hottest fields in collecting, Tarzan memorabilia ranges from comic books at a dollar or two to first editions valued in the thousands! Part of our cultural heritage for nearly a century, the chest-beating ape man (what other fictional character can be described by a gesture?) has been a hero for generations of boys and girls. Appearing in books, movies, radio, comics, toys, television, cartoons, and even on luggage and vitamins, the image of Tarzan is sure to spark childhood memories of Saturday movie matinees or evenings spent reading the latest issue Tarzan comic book. Tarzan collectibles can be found at the priciest auction house or your neighbor's yard sale. Recently a movie poster from the 1928 production Tarzan The Mighty went under the gavel for over $30,000. Many of the Tarzan cereal premiums from the '30s and '40s are today worth several hundred dollars. Tarzan comics and books (both hard cover and paperback) offer the collector a chance to obtain samples of artwork by some of the greatest illustrators, past and present. Just as the worth of vintage items grows, today's toys, comic books, movie, and other Tarzan memorabilia have the potential to increase in value.

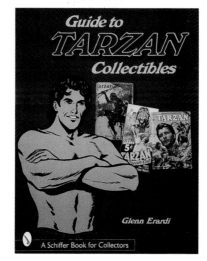

Size: 8 1/2" x 11"	479 photos	160 pp.
Price Guide		
ISBN: 0-7643-0575-1	soft cover	$29.95

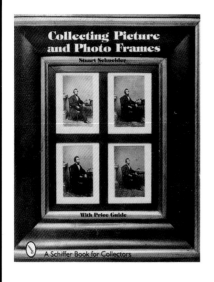

Collecting Picture and Photo Frames Stuart Schneider. Collecting Picture and Photo Frames introduces the reader to the history of frames and an across-the-board sampling of framing styles from the early 1800s through the 1940s. Beautifully illustrated in over 400 color photographs, this book is the first of its kind to show such variety and magnitude of both wall frames and table top frames in detail and full color. Whether you are an amateur or novice collector of frames, someone who simply appreciates good frames for your pictures, or a student of art and design history, this book will give you insight into the style, beauty, and value of antique frames. Different frame materials are described, along with information on identifying and dating your pieces. A price guide is also given for each item.

Size: 8 1/2"x 11"	403 color photos	176 pp.
Price Guide		Index
ISBN: 0-7643-0610-3	hard cover	$39.95

Star Trek Collectibles: Classic Series, Next Generation, Deep Space Nine, Voyager
Ursula Augustin. The televised Star Trek adventures have taken millions where no man has gone before. Perhaps this helps explain why collectibles from thirty years of "space fever" are so sought after, from the Enterprise's initial takeoff right up to the adventures of the spaceship Voyager. This unique price catalogue contains more than 1,000 collectibles, many of which sold-out long ago on the retail market and assesses their skyrocketing prices in today's collectibles universe. What's more, this unique price catalogue for old and new "space" articles presents more than 1,000 collector's pieces in gorgeous color and black and white illustrations, including highly topical Voyager collectibles from the newest Star Trek series.

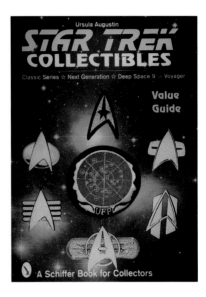

Size: 8 1/2" x 11"	1000 photos & illus.	192 pp.
Price Guide		
ISBN: 0-7643-0378-3	soft cover	$19.95

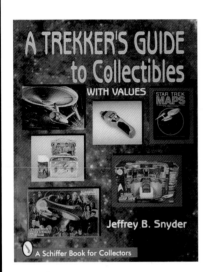

A Trekker's Guide to Collectibles with Prices Jeffrey B. Snyder. In 1996, Star Trek and the crew of the Enterprise celebrate their 30th anniversary. Today, the Star Trek world is a multi-million dollar adventure with three spin-off television series and seven movies to date with thousands of loyal fans. The mountain of collectibles Star Trek has left in its wake are presented here in text, lists of items and over 490 color photographs with captions chronicling the field. Brief synopses of the series and films put the collectibles in perspective.

Size: 8 1/2 x 11"	490 color photographs	160pp.
Price Guide		
ISBN: 0-88740-965-2	soft cover	$29.95

Collecting Star Wars Toys 1977-1997: An Unauthorized Guide Jeffrey B. Snyder. Presented here in lively text and over 650 color photographs are the toys that have been played with and collected by ardent fans of George Lucas' Star Wars trilogy for twenty years. The action figures, accessories, playsets, and spacecraft of the Rebellion and the Empire are displayed in a colorful and easily referenced format. The gaming equipment, model kits, playthings, promotional items, puzzles, and weapons produced from 1977 through 1997 are examined as well. Not stopping there, this sweeping survey includes an overview of the most popular items from the rest of the ever-expanding Star Wars collectibles universe. Prices are included in the captions; listings for toys both loose and mint-in-the-package are provided whenever appropriate. Rounding out this practical guide are a short history of science fiction films, an examination of action figures, and a bibliography.

Size: 8 1/2" x 11"	655 color photos	176 pp.
Price Guide		
ISBN: 0-7643-0651-0	soft cover	$29.95